Yesterday's Bride

Gowns, Weddings,
& Traditions
1850 to 1930

Anthony Jude Cavo

To my parents who taught me the meaning of love, the importance of justice, the necessity for compassion, the beauty in giving, the value of joy, the significance of knowledge, the ability to forgive, the love of God, the merits of truth, the cost of a lie, and the exquisiteness of mercy. You were a gift from God to us and a loss from us to God. You live in your children and theirs; thank you for life and your boundless love. Te voglio bene assai, ma tanto tanto bene sai.

A special thanks to my publishing coach, Ally Nathaniel (www.allynathaniel.com) for her guidance, patience, and for sharing her brilliance - Shalom berakhah ve-tovah.

The following full-page photograph of my parents was taken on April 26, 1952 in Brooklyn, NY.

Introduction

From bride by capture to bride by choice the history of the wedding has reflected changes in society's attitude toward women. Despite changing laws women were still considered chattel in western culture as recently as the late 19th century. Daughters could be bartered in exchange for economic or social advancement or to forge or strengthen familial or business alliances. Dowries and daughters were the prices paid to insure familial gain. Dowries and bride prices, the amount paid by a groom to a captured bride's family, go back as far as recorded time in every known major society. Although love and attraction have always been a reason for the pairing of men and women it was a practice seen more often among the poor and was not the norm among the upper classes. During tribal times and later for the working class and their wealthier counterparts, marriage was seen as an opportunity for social and financial advancement. The basis for courtship and marriage was practical rather than emotional; love was not a requirement.

The notion of love as a foundation for marriage was a radical idea until the 16th Century Elizabethans, even then it was less practical and more conceptual. Romeo and Juliet (written during this age) let their hearts rule their heads and almost anyone, literate or otherwise, can tell you the outcome of their progressive attitudes.

Yesterday's Bride recaps landmarks in the battle for the enfranchisement of women are correlated with photographs of brides during the corresponding time in history. It is interesting to note the parallels in the evolution of the women's suffrage movement and the style of clothing worn by women: from the binding, often deadly corsets of the oppressive 19th Century to the sheer, nude look of the liberating 1920s when women had their first taste of national political inclusion. It could be said that women's fashion recapitulates equality, or the contrary.

The fascinating and charming photographs in Yesterday's Bride will give you a glimpse of bridal costumes from 1858 through the 1930s and illustrate how social mores, economy, and even war have influenced fashion in general and bridal fashion specifically. In photos lacking family history and without recorded dates the period was determined by fashion, the type of photo, back drops in the photo, and even the stock upon which the photograph is mounted – all significant considerations when attributing a date. The material described for the gowns is based on verbal history, and examination of the magnified photo along with knowledge of materials popular at the time, and in some cases by direct examination of the actual gowns or remnants.

The photographs are accompanied by descriptions of wedding traditions and superstitions and their origins from the Pre-Dynastic Egyptian Period (3500 – 3050 BC), the ancient Greeks and Romans, up to some relatively modern practices. You will learn the reasons and roots of Western wedding traditions for everything from elaborate veils to the seemingly unimportant boutonniere on the groom's lapel. Some of these traditions may be new to you and you may wish to include them in your own wedding plans.

The photos, text and quotes by the famous about brides, wives, and weddings will prove to be a valued source of reference for the bride-to-be in planning her wedding, writing her ceremony, or choosing, even designing, her own gown.

_____

_____

_____

_____

_____

1860: Decade of the Hoopskirt

The hoopskirt, most often associated with Gone With the Wind, Scarlet O'Hara, and the Civil War Era dominated women's fashion from the late 1840s to the mid-1860s to the exclusion of almost every other style. These massive gowns were worn during the day and evening for informal and formal events and as wedding gowns. The colors were vibrant and the cost extravagant depending on the material utilized. They were initially given their classic shape by up to six petticoats or crinolines that were later replaced by bell-shaped cages or hoops of metal or baleen (whale bone). These undergarments and contraptions added considerable weight to the already heavy dresses composed of many yards of material; the petticoats alone could weigh up to fifteen pounds. A complete typical outfit of the time could weigh in excess of thirty pounds. The fancy skirts that covered the hoops or petticoats typically had hemlines with a circumference of fifteen feet or more. The amount of material in a bodice could range from three to four yards, and up to eight to ten yards of material for the skirt alone. Furniture designed during this era was tailored to suit this style. Chairs of all types were made with low arms (demi-arms) or no arms to accommodate these voluminous skirts (chairs for men continued to have arms) and women not only had to learn to sit, they had to learn how to pass through doors, kneel, and contend with the wind without exposing their undergarments.

Wedding gowns were not exempt from the fashion excesses of the time. Indeed, wedding gowns mimicked the style of the day in every way; however, wedding gowns were white or off-white with like-color trim. Many brides, shunning the extravagance and impractical nature of a white gown chose to marry in their best dress, often vibrant in color, while donning a white veil trimmed in wax orange buds and blossoms.

By the end of the decade the front of the hoopskirt began to flatten out with the aid of tapes and drawstrings leaving a more elliptical shape with the fullness concentrated at the back – a foreshadowing of the bustles of the 1870s.

Hoopskirts are underskirts with rings of metal or whalebone of varying circumferences sewn in at intervals with the narrowest at the top and widest at the bottom.

Petticoats are underskirts that add fullness to a gown. Some petticoats were very elaborate and were meant to be worn with open-front skirts.

Crinolines are underskirts of fabric stiffened by using horsehair in the weave. The word "crine" is Italian for horsehair.

Why White?

White has long been the color that symbolized purity and virginity, although in Biblical times the color of choice for virgins was blue. In ancient times, however, white material symbolized wealth, as it was a long and costly process to bleach cloth to a pure white color. Even during the early twentieth century when white material became less expensive and more available a white dress still represented wealth. The average woman seldom had the opportunity or occasion to wear white, which, in the days of washing garments by hand, was not practical for everyday use. A bride would have to be a woman of substance to afford the frivolity of a white gown.

When Anne of Brittany married Louis XII of France in 1466 (her third marriage) she wore white, a fashion that remained popular for a short period of time before falling out of favor for more brightly colored and embroidered gowns. Wedding gowns during the sixteenth, seventeenth and eighteenth centuries continued to be colorful. In 1840 Queen Victoria chose a plain cream silk wedding gown in place of the heavily jeweled and embroidered gowns previously worn by royalty for her marriage to Prince Albert. It took more than 200 workers nine months to complete the lace required for Victoria's gown. Fashion magazines and newspapers of the day carried the details of the wedding along with a description of the gown and as simply as that, white was again the chosen color for wedding gowns.

A style that remained popular throughout the late 1840s, 1850s and early 1860s is the hoop skirt seen on this early Victorian bride who wears a simple yet elegant hoop skirt of silk taffeta with a sweep train. The bride's tulle veil is attached to a crown of wax orange buds and blossoms; a corsage of the same is worn on the fitted bodice. It is of interest to note that this style, often having a hem with a circumference of 15 feet or more, would be repeated 100 years later during the late 1950's and early 1960's. Maneuvering through doorways was difficult, and it was not unusual for women wearing these gowns with their stiff wire hoops to knock over small furniture or even little children.

"What is thine is mine, and all mine is thine." Marcus Tullius Cicero (106 – 43 B.C.)

A bodice is the upper part of a dress, either separate from, or attached to the skirt. It is often enhanced by a skirt-like addition, known as a basque, which covers the hips.

1870: The Bustle Appears

The hoopskirt disappeared by 1869 when fullness in skirts shifted to the back of the skirt became a large bustle. Skirts and underskirts became straight, narrow and tight and were ornately, even ostentatiously embellished. Gaudy displays of unusual trimming, pleating, ruffles, flounces, bows, ribbons, buttons, fringe, puffs, and extraordinary methods of draping were utilized. Bright, startling colors were now available with the introduction of new aniline dyes. The outrageous designs and styles were limited only by the designer's imagination. One of the most popular styles of the 1870s was the polonaise, a single garment from shoulder to hem that incorporated a bodice and a split-front overskirt drawn back on each side in panniers then gathered and trained behind; it was essentially a bodice with a very long basque. Trains, often with a balayeuse, were seen on all fashionable dresses and were considered short if less than twenty inches dragged behind. The excessive amount of garniture and enormous amount of material used in the dresses of this period made the garments outrageously expensive and created the perfect opportunity to display one's wealth.

By 1875 the bustle began to diminish in size until the end of the decade when it was little more than a small pad. Skirts became tighter from hip to hem, which limited each step to about six inches, but they retained their trains, giving the dress a fish-tail appearance.

A bustle, made of a framework of steel, wire, or horsehair, is a visor-shaped undergarment worn at the base of the spine in order to accentuate the shape of the backside.

A bodice is the upper part of a dress either separate from or attached to the skirt. It is often enhanced by a skirt-like addition known as a basque, which covers the hips.

Panniers are festoons formed by elaborate draping of a skirt over the hips. The shape of the panniers was often maintained by a wire framework and served to accentuate the fullness of the hips.

A balayeuse is a removable dust ruffle tacked beneath the train of a gown that prevents the material of the train from dragging directly against the floor.

During the eighteenth and nineteenth century shoes for brides were typically made of silk, satin, or kid. The tight-fitting, lace-up wedding boots on the previous page date from 1890 to 1900 and are made of white kid. They are almost a foot tall, have forty eyelets each, and spool heels; one of the most popular heels at the time. The laces were pulled tight with a hook at the level of each pair of eyelets and putting them on took some effort and more than a little time. Shoes from this period were typically small compared to today; the average shoe size for a woman during this time was 3.5 to 4. Small, narrow feet were so desirable it was not uncommon for women to have their pinky toe amputated to attain such an appearance; not unlike the "stiletto surgery" of today.

During this time in many parts of the United States once a woman married she effectively surrendered unto her husband any rights to property she owned prior to her marriage. She also surrendered the right to bring lawsuits, sell or transfer property, make contracts, or control any income – including any income that belong to her as a single woman. All women, whether married or single, did not have the right to vote.

In 1869, just about the time this bride took her vows, Elizabeth Cady Stanton and Susan B. Anthony formed the NWSA (National Woman's Suffrage Association). In the same year another woman, Julia Ward, along with Lucy Stone and her husband, Henry Blackwell, established the AWSA (American Women's Suffrage Association). Both groups, composed of men and women, campaigned for political enfranchisement of women.

Elaborate, overly adorned gowns epitomized the look of the 1870s and wedding gowns, as seen in this a classic example, were not exempt from these fashion excesses.

This bride wears a polonaise in which the bodice and draped overskirt are one piece. The tight fitting bodice dips well below the hips, has a lace fraise collar, and a diagonally draped and gathered sash. It is drawn up behind to form lace-trimmed, festooned panniers and a low bustle which falls into a flounced chapel-length train with ruching and ruffles; flowers, pleated ruffles, lace trim, and puffs decorate the instep-length underskirt. Pale hyacinths (loveliness and youth) decorate the bodice and there is a posy of fresh wild flowers pinned at her waist.

The tulle veil, which sits back on her head, is gathered at the nape of the neck by a cluster of tiny white flowers. On the table along with her prayer book are her fan and an elaborate music or jewel box – possibly a gift from the groom.

Panniers, the French word for a pair of baskets or saddle bags, refer to a puffed arrangement of drapery at the hips either freely draping or supported by a wire or stiffened material infrastructure.

Wife or Servant?

An ancient Hindu code, more than four thousand years old, states that, "A man, both day and night, must keep his wife so much in subjection that she by no means be mistress of her own actions. If the wife have her own free will, notwithstanding she be of a superior caste, she will behave amiss."

It is difficult to imagine that over four thousand years later the sentiments about wives and marriage hadn't changed very much. Consider the following quotes:

"The husband hath by law, power and dominion over his wife, and may keep her by force, within the bounds of duty, and may beat her, but not in a violent or cruel manner."
Sir Francis Bacon, English philosopher and writer (1561 – 1626)

"The first and most important quality of a woman is sweetness. She must learn to submit uncomplainingly to unjust treatment and marital wrongs."
Jean Jacques Rosseau, Philosopher and writer (1712 – 1778)

"By marriage the husband and the wife are one person in law; that is, the very being or legal existence of the woman is suspended during the marriage, or at least is incorporated and consolidated into that of her husband."
Sir William Blackstone's Commentaries on the Laws of England 1765

"...the husband and the wife are regarded as one person, and her legal existence and authority lost or suspended during the continuance of the matrimonial union."
James Kent (1763 – 1847), Chief Justice of the Supreme Court

"The wife is only the servant of her husband." Baron Alderson, 19th Century Judge

This demure looking bride, married on October 20, 1875, is dressed in a gown of white, which had, by this time, become traditional. Reflective poses and expressions are typical of Victorian photographs and the Victorian's romanticized notion of love and serious regard for the sacrament of marriage.

Rain or Shine

Many people believe that rain on your wedding day is an omen of bad luck to come, yet others believe that rain, needed to replenish and sustain all life, is a blessing on your wedding day and that if you are a bride upon whom it rains you will live a happy, productive life filled with good fortune and many children.

A method, according to many Catholics, that guarantees a sunny wedding day, or at least to prevent rain during the ceremony, is to hang rosary beads out of the window or on the clothesline the night before the wedding.

This bride of the late 1870s wears a long basque bodice and a narrow overskirt that is cinched behind in a large boxed pleat to form an elaborate, gathered, cathedral-length train under which can be seen the balayeuse (a lining that could easily be removed for cleaning or replacing), and an intricately shirred and fringed underskirt with ruching.

The tulle cathedral-length veil sits back on her head and is fastened by a large decorative crown of cascading wax orange blossoms and buds; a fancy corsage of wax orange blossoms complements the headpiece and she carries a Tussie Mussie of delphinium and sweet pea (heavenly light and bliss).

"Happy the bride the sun shines on" is an ancient and widely held superstition. The photographer's elaborate trompe l'oeil background with streaming artificial sunlight ensures a happy married life for this bride regardless of the weather outside his studio

A basque bodice is a tightly fitted bodice, sometimes having an extension that covers the hips.

A Tussie Mussie is a small bouquet of flowers commonly known as a nosegay. It also describes the small cone-shaped holder for these nosegays.

1880: The Bustle Returns

By the late 1870s the bustle had diminished in size to a small cushion, but by 1887 the bustle was back and bigger than it had been during the previous decade. The shape of the bustle was much more exaggerated and had a shelf-like appearance that ballooned out horizontally from behind. A very fashionable woman of the day would resemble a Centaur in a gown, or an expensively dressed woman with a horse's rump. Many people of the day joked that the large mesa-like protuberance could serve as the perfect place for a woman to carry her market basket,

The skirts remained narrow and straight but were more simply decorated and featured asymmetrical draping. Extraordinarily fitted bodices, tightly laced corsets, tiny waists and smooth round hips gave the woman a rigid, tightly wrapped appearance. By the end of the decade the bustle again disappeared and decorative emphasis shifted to the bodice which was beginning to show a slight elevation at the top of the sleeve; a hint of things to come.

Illustrations from Godey's Lady's Book 1887 and Le Beau Monde 1875 show the Victorian's attraction to the ever-growing bustle. Women of the day had to be quite adroit at maneuvering through rooms without knocking items from table-tops; sitting was also something that took practice. Wedding dresses were no exception from this style excess. It appears that it was "all about that bass" long before Meghan Trainor bought booty back.

Orange Blossoms

The use of orange blossoms as a wedding ornament comes directly from Greek mythology with the wedding of Hera, goddess of marriage, and Zeus, the king of heaven. Hera was presented with orange blossoms on her wedding night by Gaea, the goddess of earth and fertility. Orange blossoms also figured in a very famous mythological Roman wedding, that of Juno, queen of heaven and protector of women, and her marriage to Jupiter, the supreme Roman deity.

Orange blossoms come from a unique evergreen tree that blossoms and bears fruit at the same time, and in all seasons. No wonder it has remained as an enduring symbol of beauty, fertility, and love. Today we owe our fascination with orange blossoms to Queen Victoria who, during her wedding, wore elaborate Turkish diamond earrings and matching necklace with a large sapphire and diamond brooch, but chose, in place of any number of jeweled tiaras, a simple circlet of orange blossoms to fasten her veil.

In 1880 this San Francisco bride with the far away, wistful expression dressed in an exceedingly fashionable silk ensemble; a luxury very few women could afford.

According to style her tulle veil sits back on her forehead to reveal a ringlet of fringed hair (a frise) and sausage curls. These curls were achieved by a variety of means. One interesting method was to wind the hair around wood cylinders then coat it with sugar water. When the hair was dry, the form was removed, and the curl remained. The train is cathedral-length as is the veil, which is fastened by a large crown of wax orange blossoms that also gather the veil behind the neck. Another cluster of orange blossoms is worn at her throat.

Rings adorn her second and fourth left fingers and a wide, ornate cuff bracelet is worn on her left wrist. Her bouquet of pale roses (romance, love, tenderness) and myrtle leaves (love, fertility, youth, peace, and wedded bliss), sits on the table.

In 1880 women in Vermont, New York, and Mississippi won partial suffrage.

"Love bears all things, believes all things, hopes all things, endures all things."
The Bible: 1 Corinthians

Suffrage, in short, is the right to vote. Partial suffrage describes voting rights that are limited to: school board elections, municipal elections, or state elections for women of certain classes.

During the nineteenth century, western wedding apparel rapidly spread to all parts of the world, especially those countries within the British Empire. The new Mrs. Williamson, married in Bombay, chose to wear a wedding costume that would have been up to the moment in Europe and the United States, complete with the de rigueur wax orange buds and blossoms. Her veil and gown bear no resemblance to the traditional Indian wedding attire of the 1880s. The pose is almost exactly the same as the American couple in the previous photograph taken during the same time period.

The only concession made to Indian fashion can be seen in Mr. Williamson's clothing; he wears a Nehru shirt and Nehru vest. Mr. Williamson was a Preventive Officer (Customs Agent) in Her Majesty Queen Victoria's Customs, Bombay.

A traditional Hindu wedding includes three very charming rituals called: Kanyadaan, Panigrahana, and Saptapadi. Kanyadaan is the part of the ceremony where the father of the bride gives away his daughter. Panigrahana involves the groom taking the bride's hand in the presence of fire as a symbol of their union, The bride is seated and looking east with the groom standing looking west while the groom announces his acceptance of the responsibilities of marriage to four gods: one god denoting wealth, one god representing the heavens, one god symbolizing radiance and a new beginning, and the last god denoting wisdom. Saptadpadi is the most important part of the ceremony and the part that makes the ceremony legal. The couple walks around the fire (which serves as witness to their union) seven times each holding the other's right hand or with part of their clothing tied together. With each turn the couple recites vows. Typically the bride leads the groom for the first circuit and sometimes the first three or five circuits with the groom leading for the balance; the order is determined by the region in which the couple lives.

Bridal Shower

The origin of the bridal shower is not very clear. Some research indicates that the bridal shower, as we know it today, began in Holland during the seventeenth century when a miller denied consent for his daughter to marry a man who hadn't the means to provide all that was necessary to set up house for his beloved. The girl was so broken-hearted that her friends and women of the town converged on her home each with a useful household object. Thus equipped, the father could no longer withhold his consent and the couple was married. The term "shower," however, did not take hold until the waning years of the Victorian era when an engaged woman's friends would fill a Japanese parasol with small gifts that showered her when she opened the parasol over her head. If you desire to revive this charming tradition it is not recommended you try it with irons, toasters, carving knives or blenders.

Elaborate draping, ribbons, ruffles, trim, yards of lace, and a gathered train seen in this polonaise of the late 1870s to early 1880s typifies the embellishments favored by women at that time. The skirt is closely fitted at the front and gathered behind in folds to form a fancy, long, chapel-to-cathedral-length train with rows of pleats and ruffles; the hem is drawn up with ribbons to reveal a heavily pleated underskirt. This gown is an example of the type of gown that would have been worn by a wealthy woman for her wedding or fancy ball.

The woman in this photo is California native Mary Anderson, a famous, red-haired beauty admired by Americans and the British for her fine acting, great beauty, and charitable deeds.

In 1881 the American branch of the Red Cross was established and Clara Barton became its first president. In that same year, Harriet Giles and Sara Packard opened Spelman College, a school for black women, in Atlanta, Georgia.

So popular was the plumage of the ostrich, egret, bird-of-paradise, and other brightly colored birds that some species, particularly the egret and bird-of-paradise, were hunted to the brink of extinction. The feathers were used to trim garments and make fans. The plumes were especially prized to adorn the fancy hats favored by most women of the day. Indeed, it was not uncommon to see a massive hat sporting not only the feathers but the entire bird itself.

The gown seen on this bride from the early 1880s appears quite simple at first glance, however, closer inspection reveals the elaborate detailing. The fitted basque bodice has a fashionable square neckline decorated by pearl-studded lace and strung-pearl tassels which end at waist-length.

The floral pattern damassé skirt has large box pleating at each side and is decorated with pearl tasseled appliqué - the topmost serving as an agraffe on the large box pleat. The skirt is gathered in the back to form a long, puffed cathedral-length train that is probably filled with lamb's wool; a finely pleated underskirt is visible.

She carries a large ostrich plume fan and adorns her hair with a panache of ostrich and egret plumes; she wears simple pearl-drop earrings. During the 1890s and early 1900s many brides chose to wear the stylish aigrette or a fashionable hat in place of the traditional veil.

Bryn Mawr College Founded in 1885 by Joseph Taylor, a Quaker, was the first woman's institution to offer graduate degrees including a Ph.D.

Aigrette is the French word for egret, a small white heron that was relentlessly hunted during the late nineteenth to early twentieth centuries for its plumage, most particularly the long branching plumes of the head, neck and back that cascade during mating season. The plumage was used in women's hats and headdresses, very often tucked into elaborate coiffures or head bands. The term has come to apply to any upwardly projecting adornment attached to a hat or the hair. Many of these aigrettes contain no feathers at all and take the form of a comb with sprays of beautifully faceted quartz, paste or precious gems.

Luck

A torn veil, beggars, black cats, lambs, doves, and chimney sweeps (especially if one kisses you) are all considered great luck for a bride to encounter. Finding a spider (symbolic of industry, skill and success) in or on her wedding gown denotes an extra special dose of fortune. Marriage during a waxing moon is considered fortuitous, whereas marriage during a waning moon is not. It was believed that a bride could solicit good luck by: wearing gold earrings, entering and leaving the church on her right foot, feeding a cat out of her wedding shoe, wearing something old, new, borrowed, and blue, and sewing a penny or silver coin in the hem of her wedding dress, or placing it in her shoe.

In the Jewish culture, a gift of any sharp object to a bride, especially a knife, is considered bad luck. If a bride is given such an object she can ward off the evil by turning the gift into a business transaction by "paying" a penny to the person who gave the gift.

Despite the popularity of the white wedding dress many women, in order to avoid the cost and frivolity of a white gown, still wore their best dress when they married. Bright shades of blue, green, purple, rich browns and even red were favored. It is likely that this bride from the late 1880s is wearing one such color. A veil, bouquet, or a simple corsage of orange blossoms is often the only evident displays that a photo is of a bride and her groom.

An elaborate crown of flowers sits high atop this bride's head and gives rise to a waltz-length tulle veil; she wears a similar sprig of flowers at her throat and carries a beribboned Tussie Mussie of snapdragons (strength) and lace.

In 1887 women in Arizona, Montana, New Jersey, North Dakota, and South Dakota won partial suffrage; the same year, women in Utah lose their limited voting rights. The following year, in 1888, the International Council of Women held its first meeting.

"It takes two flints to make a fire." Louisa May Alcott (1832 – 1888)

1890: The Hourglass Figure

A walk up the aisle didn't mean a woman had to surrender the fashionable styles of her day. Trends in fashion have always managed to find their way into wedding couture and the decade from 1890 to 1900 was no exception. The silhouette most keenly associated with the 1890s was the hourglass figure: a tiny waist, smooth, round hips, swirling gored skirts, and massive balloon sleeves did not actually take shape until the mid-1890s and lasted only a short time. The effect, however, was so dramatic that the style has come to epitomize the entire decade.

Early in the 1890s skirts remained narrow, gathered and draped mush as they had been during the late 1880s. Soon, however, the skirt, although still smooth and fitted at the hip became full and swirling at the base with the help of gored panels. These panels of material, narrow at the top and wide at the bottom, were inset from the thigh down, resulting in a very full skirt with deep umbrella folds and a circumference at the hemline of five to seven yards. The swirling skirts were lined with stiff silk taffeta that together with the popular taffeta underskirts, rustled in a way that many men described as very enticing. The rustling sound was so popular it was even given a name – frou-frou.

A slight rise at the top of the sleeve early in the decade was merely a hint of things to come. The shoulders, often adorned with epaulets, initially showed a slight fullness at the shoulder and upper arm, but by 1895 the top of the sleeve at the shoulder grew to such an enormous size that passing through the average doorway was accomplished only by deft maneuvering. Sleeves of such monumental proportions required up to three yards of material for a pair and maintained their size and shape with the support of cotton wadding or stiffened inner linings of material such as taffeta or muslin. These large, popular sleeves, often with vertical pleating, could be seen in a variety of shapes: balloon, leg of mutton, melon, or gigot. As the shoulders grew in width so did the hemline of the skirt in an attempt at maintaining a visual balance. The tiny waist was emphasized by fancy cummerbunds of pleated silk or satin called girdles. Bodices were bloused and draped with bibs or jabots of lace, and though still tightly corseted the blousing effect gave the illusion of a looser, lighter, less encumbering, less confining bodice.

High, stiff collars or neckbands remained popular throughout the decade although evening gowns and some bridal gowns displayed low necklines. Massive hats were required in order to compete with the bell-shaped skirts and broad shoulders. In place of the traditional veil many brides wore these massive hats generously decorated with orange blossoms, veiling, lace, plumes, bows, flowers and often an entire stuffed bird.

The cake topper on the previous page is from the early 1920s. It is made of cloth, tulle, and crepe paper. Crepe paper cake toppers were popular during the early twentieth century from about 1900 through the 1920s. Other popular themes were ceramic or celluloid Cupie dolls with crepe paper clothing with the bride and groom often being identical except for the outfits. Cupids and cardboard cutouts were also very popular during that time. It wasn't unusual to have additional members of the bridal party represented in the cake toppers of the 1920s.

I don't, I don't; I guess I do.

Weddings were not always the romantic occasions we celebrate today. Throughout most of recorded history, and presumably before that, women had little to say with regard to which man they married. Bride by capture was one of the most common methods an ancient groom employed in his acquisition of a wife. The woman was simply taken from another village or even a family living in his own town. Once captured, she was not given the opportunity to say "I don't" - she had no choice. After the wedding had taken place and the marriage consummated the captive woman was considered the captor's wife and property and eventually her family (who more than likely obtained wives by the same method) had to come to terms with this state of affairs. The bride's father then stated his terms or bride price to be paid by the groom. In 866 A.D. the Christian church renounced this practice and Pope Nicholas I deemed that if consent to marriage was lacking, even if the union was consummated, the marriage was void. This did little to change the course for the captive bride. Most women opted to remain with their "husbands" once the "marriage" was consummated as they were no longer considered marriageable as a result of their non-virgin state. This is the same pope who in 860 A. D. decreed that nuptial intent had to be marked by a gold ring. Investing something as valuable as a gold ring guaranteed that men were less likely to glibly enter into a marriage contract. If he broke the contract he forfeited the ring, if she broke the contract the ring had to be returned.

Simple, smooth lines and a rich glossy fabric of lustrous white silk satin with a high, stand up, horizontally tucked collar establish this bride of the early 1890s as a woman of taste, wealth, and fashion. The tight, full-length, shirred sleeves are puffed at the top and have ruching at the cuff. Her straight, smooth, gored skirt is gathered in pleats at the back to form a cathedral-length train. Silk tulle cathedral-length veiling is attached at the crown of her head by a headdress of wax orange blossoms and buds. She wears a satin-bow corsage with wax orange blossoms and a posy of the same at her waist. Her bouquet consists of one half dozen dark roses (deep love) and fern (wisdom, fascination).

During this time arranged marriages, though rapidly falling out of favor, were still arranged in the sense that the bride's father had to approve of the man she intended to marry, and very often found a man whom he encouraged her to marry. Did this bride marry the man she loved, or, as did many women of her generation, marry the man deemed most suitable or advantageous?

In 1889 Barnard College is opened and in 1890 women in Oklahoma and Washington State won partial suffrage and Wyoming becomes a state with full suffrage for women.

As the populace became more "civilized," gaining a bride by capture became taboo and it would be reassuring to think the restrictions against taking a bride by force were based on such ideal principles as morality and justice. It's likely, however, that the ban on brides by capture developed as a means of protecting one man's property (daughters) against another man's covetousness. As a result of these laws, single women were considered the property of their fathers until they married and it was he who decided when and whom she would marry. His decision was based on a form of barter – his daughter and her dowry in exchange for a secure alliance, the better the alliance the larger the dowry. Prospective husbands were considered and the one from whom the bride, and her family, would gain the most, whether in social rank, wealth or merging of businesses, was chosen.

Until Elizabethan times the notion of romance did not signify in marriage. The prevailing attitude toward marriage was one of practicality as expressed in this quote by American novelist, essayist, and critic James Branch Cabell, "People marry for a variety of reasons and with varying results. But to marry for love is to invite inevitable tragedy."

In the United States arranged marriages, somewhat modified to allow for romance, continued well into the nineteenth century. Although, by the late 18th century the increasing number of women who were pregnant before their walk down the aisle superseded any arrangement a woman's father cared to make.

It is not uncommon to see photographs of seemingly unhappy brides, or couples who appear not only to be strangers, but downright confused and afraid. When a man asks his girlfriend's father for permission to marry, it is a practice having more to do with tradition rather than exchange. This practice, however, has roots in the not-so-distant past when a single woman was deemed property. A derivative of that practice is the question asked by the person officiating at the ceremony, "Who gives this woman in marriage?" Arranged marriages and marriage by barter continue today in many countries throughout the world.

This bride wears a simple, court-train gown of white silk organdy with a slight rise at the top of the sleeves, indicative of a gown from the early 1890s. She is literally garnished with garlands of myrtle leaves (*love, fertility, youth, peace, wedded bliss*), and tulips (*perfect love*). Her ankle-length silk tulle veil is gathered into a crown at the top and fastened by a trailing garland of tiny white flowers and myrtle leaves.

The apparent lack of intimacy between the newly married couple in this early 1890s photograph is surprising by today's standards and suggests they have only recently become acquainted, which may or may not be true, but the strict moral code and mores of the Victorian era extended even to photography.

The traditional wedding pose up until this time was one in which both the bride and groom were standing, or more commonly one in which the groom sat and the bride stood to the side and slightly behind, suggestive of the bride's subordination to, and attendance upon the groom. This photo is unusual in that the posturing of the bride and groom are reversed. It would be encouraging to think the groom's sense of chivalry was stronger than his sense of dominance; however, the seating arrangement is more than likely a result of the bride's height. A wedding photo in which the bride stands taller than the groom would hardly be acceptable at that time, and would invite comment and supposition. By standing, this groom expresses his dominance.

A white gown with a V-neck, and a loose fitting, slightly draped bodice that is shirred at the shoulders to form loose, vertical folds exaggerates the width of the torso and narrowness of the waist, which is further enhanced by the use of a girdle.* The bodice buttons down the center and is decorated by three large bows. A silk chemisette fills in the V-neck and forms a high collar of horizontally tucked silk.

The bride's intricately braided hair is decorated with small silk flowers and a tiara inside of which fine tulle is gathered before forming a floor-length veil. She carries a posy of tiny wild flowers tied with ribbon and streamers of the same material as her gown.

*The wide belts and sashes popular at the close of the 19th century and beginning of the 20th century were often referred to as girdles.

"Marrying for love may be a bit risky, but it is so honest that God can't help but smile on it." Josh Billings (1818 – 1885)

In ancient Ireland brides and grooms exchanged bracelets, or less often rings, made of their braided hair as symbols of their betrothal or engagement. This hair jewelry was also used as wedding rings. During the Victorian era it was quite common for the bride to present her groom with a gift of a fancy watch chain or fob made from a lock of her finely woven hair. These gifts were often composed of intertwined locks of the bride's and groom's hair, and men frequently bestowed rings or bracelets made of their own hair to their fiancés. Both men and women gave and received lockets containing their true loves' hair.

During the early 1890s Adele posed for this wedding photo in an off-white, fashionable gown of rich silk taffeta. The loose-fitting bodice is decorated with a large, fancy, asymmetrical bib of intricate pearl-studded swirled panels and frills of lace. Double-capped sleeves of lace and satin top the puff sleeves, which are shirred to the elbow and fitted from elbow to wrist. The collar is high with six rows of finely tucked silk; a silk sash tied in a bow on the left encircles the cinched waist.

The smooth, gored skirt ends in a square, puffed, cathedral-length train with frills and ruching. Trains were often puffed and shaped by down or lamb's wool filling.

It was not uncommon for the Victorian bride to be photographed without her veil or flowers. Not only did the veil hide the hair, which was often elaborately arranged, the voluminous veiling and immense bouquets often obscured the bride's dress.

To be married before the age of 21 with a waist size less than your age was the aspiration of most women up until the 1920s. Note Emma's tiny waist, made even narrower by tightly laced corsets; a fashion for which women literally died. As a result of corseting at an early age, as early as birth in some cultures, many women developed deformities of the spine, ribs, and internal viscera; near normal breaths were almost impossible. Common side effects of this unnatural binding of the female form were numerous including numbness of the lower extremities and fainting with the woman being revived by cutting of the corset laces. Intestinal strangulation and death were not uncommon.

In 1892 Emma Wild (a very determined looking woman) chose for her wedding a traditional, corseted, basque bodice, fashioned after the bodices worn by Basque peasants. The bodice is covered by a sheer tulle shell and decorated with frills of dotted Swiss at the cuffs.

The silk tulle veil is gathered atop her head where it is fastened by a large cluster of wax orange blossoms; garlands of wax orange blossoms trail from the crown to the bride's bust. She holds a long, interesting garland of white flowers at her left hip and wears a corsage of wax orange buds and blossoms.

"A wedding anniversary is the celebration of love, trust, partnership, tolerance and tenacity. The order varies for any given year." Paul Sweeney

Wedding Cake

The wedding cake has been an intrinsic part of the wedding tradition since ancient times. Small wheat cakes were broken over the bride's head as signs of luck and fertility. Guests also took small wheat cakes to the wedding reception where they were piled in a high pyramid over which the bride and groom would kiss. Someone had the brilliant idea of icing these pyramids and that soon developed into the wedding cake we know today.

Horseshoes, long considered symbols of good luck, were often carried in the bride's bouquet or in the groom's pocket. In later years the real horseshoe gave way to facsimiles in the form of stickpins, brooches, and watch fobs.

The inclusion of the wedding cake in this couple's wedding photo from 1893 is quite remarkable, even if it is a photo-studio prop. Unlike today, wedding cakes were not, as a rule, photographed. The cake sits upon a glass cake stand decorated by a cut paper fringe. The figure atop the cake is a winged angel with a highly detailed costume and features; she is holding a "luck" engraved horseshoe that supports a horseshoe-shaped garland of flowers.

This bespectacled bride wears her best, a pale gown with a tightly corseted basque bodice and large-puffed sleeves that are gathered at the elbow and end in long, free-hanging net lace to the wrist. The same net lace forms a wide collar that falls into a free-hanging jabot on the tightly corseted basque bodice, which in turn is edged in a very deep fringe of net lace that drapes the hips. The smooth, full skirt is trained and adorned at the bottom with a wide band of trim, which appears to be pot lace. She wears a shallow brimmed, pinch-back hat decorated with tall silk orchids.

In 1893, Martha Carey and Mary Garrett donated funding in order to open Johns Hopkins Medical School and insisted upon equal admissions for women and men. In the same year full suffrage is granted to women in Colorado, and partial suffrage is granted to women in Connecticut. New Zealand, in 1893, became the first country to grant women their right to vote in national elections, a right not yet obtained by this bride or any women in the United States, Canada, Great Britain, or any other nation.

Pearls

To many ancient civilizations pearls symbolized the moon and were believed to be moonbeams that fell into the ocean and were swallowed by oysters. The pearl was believed to have magical powers that would ensure prosperity and a long life to the wearer. Pearls have been linked with the ancient Greek and Roman goddesses of love, Aphrodite and Venus, and have long symbolized love and marital happiness. Some cultures believe that pearls on a bride bring bad luck and that for every pearl a bride wears her husband will give her reason to cry

Sometime during the early to mid-1890s Martha married Herman in Milwaukee, Wisconsin wearing a glossy, smooth, raw silk fabric that provides lustrous definition and shimmer to the flat surfaces and beautifully highlights each fold.

Martha's snug, tightly fitted bodice is trimmed with pearls, as is the high smooth collar. A vertically pleated false yoke effect is given by pearl studded trim, which drapes in two freely hanging pearl studded panels on either side of a deep, V-shaped pearl fringe that extends from breast to waist. Her cathedral-length tulle veil is adorned by a wide panel of lace in a floral pattern

In 1894 women in Iowa and Ohio win partial suffrage and women in New Jersey lose the same right.

"Marriage is that relation, between man and woman, in which the independence is equal, the dependence mutual, and the obligations reciprocal." Louis Kaufman Anspacher

Boutonniere

It was, and still is, common practice for the groom to wear a flower from the bride's bouquet. This romantic tradition goes back to medieval days when men honored women by wearing a "token of favor" that could have been any personal item of the woman's ranging from a flower to a piece of her clothing; handkerchiefs, scarves, and even sleeves were popular tokens. The men wore these favors, often into battle, as a sign that their inspiration came from the woman who bestowed her favor. Henceforward, he was the woman's champion and in her service to defend and proclaim her beauty and honor; such is the ancestry of the little boutonniere.

At last we begin to see photographic evidence of a degree of intimacy between a bride and her groom. This bride's intricately braided, floral-decorated hair, together with a gathered-tulle puff fastened by the same garlands, forms a stylized crown to give this bride a regal appearance. Her tightly fitted basque bodice rides up high over the hips and falls to a deep point at the front. The large gathered, puffed, balloon sleeves, popular in the mid-1890s, are tightly fitted from below the puff to the wrist. She wears white satin slippers with bows at the vamp; the train and veil appear to be cathedral-length.

The lily of the valley in her hair symbolizes virtue, return of happiness and, to many Catholics, tears of the Virgin Mary. The roses in her corsage and bouquet are symbolic of romance and pure love, while the fern is symbolic of fascination and wisdom. Her groom wears a boutonniere of the same.

In 1896 full suffrage was won by women in Idaho and Utah, which brought the number of states with full voting privileges for women to a total of four. Wyoming was the first state with full voting rights for women in 1869 and Colorado the second state in 1893.

"With this ring I thee wed, with my body I thee worship, and with all my worldly goods I thee endow." The Book of Common Prayer

The Veil

The veil, originated by the Romans, was a method devised to protect the bride by confusing and interfering with the malevolence of wicked spirits or the evil eye of jealous rivals. The veil was often so dense and difficult to see through that the bride had to be escorted to her groom and literally given away. The bridesmaids dressed in costumes similar or identical to the bride's for the same reason. In later years, Anglo Saxon bridesmaids were also veiled and dressed like the bride for the purposes of confusing malignant spirits as well as the captive bride's family, or to prevent a rival to the groom from capturing the bride for his own; and modern brides think planning a wedding is tough.

When George Washington's future son-in-law came to call on George's daughter, Nellie, he saw her through a lace-curtained window and remarked to her how beautiful she looked thus adorned. She surprised him by wearing a veil of lace for their wedding and so is credited with starting that tradition.

This bride and her attendants exemplify the Victorian image of a bridal party in 1897. White gowns, long a symbol of virtue and purity, had by this time become established as traditional for brides. The psyche knot, a hairstyle popular during the early to late 1890s, can be seen on the heads of the bride and the two attendants standing to her left. A fancy comb or feathers, often decorated this knot or twist of hair.

The bride's silk gown has a box-pleated basque bodice that is tucked within a natural waistline defined by a narrow cummerbund. Fringe, tassels, and a large lace frill decorate the puckered and dimpled yoke and her stand-up collar is composed of four graduated horizontal tucks. The sleeves have large puffs at the shoulders and are fitted from below the puff to the wrist; she wears white gloves. Her silk skirt is smooth and gored and has a long, puffed cathedral train (note the balayeuse, or dust ruffle, seen within the folds of the train); the veil is also cathedral-length.

The attendants wear identical gowns, a practice popular in ancient Greece and Rome, but one that fell out of favor until its strong revival during the 1890s.

This eye-catching wedding party of 1898 exemplifies the look of the waning Victorian era: large wedding parties, large bouquets, large sleeves, and large hats. The bride wears a beautiful, trained gown of silk charmeuse and mousseline de soie. Her silk, surplice bodice has a fan collar, long shirred sleeves, and is filled in with a chemisette of shirred mousseline de soie. The skirt is full, gored, and has a puffed cathedral-length-train under which a ruffle-edged balayeuse can be seen. There are two floor-length, patterned-silk gauze sashes with large tassels decorating the skirt from waist to hem. A cluster of orange blossoms fastens the tulle waltz-length veil with blusher to the back of her head. She wears a cluster of orange blossoms on her right shoulder, and her waterfall bouquet is of lace, sage (*wisdom*), flowering vines (*fidelity*), and fern (*wisdom*).

Her bridesmaids wear bloused, heavily ruffled, silk voile bodices and long, slim, gored skirts. The skirts are decorated by intricate passementerie (trimming of braid, cord, or bead in a variety of forms) and are belted by passementerie "girdles" and sashes with long dark tassels. They wear small bolero-like jackets with shirred organza sleeves and more intricate, highly detailed passementerie of two different designs.

Their enormous silk hats are heavily plumed. They wear gloves and carry unique beribboned, circular (*eternity*) topiary wheels of ivy (*fidelity and friendship in adversity*).

In 1898, as this bride planned her wedding, women and men in Delaware and Louisiana fight for and win partial suffrage for women.

"Love feels no burden, thinks nothing of trouble, attempts what is above its own strength, pleads no excuse of impossibility; for it thinks all things lawful for itself, and all things possible. It is therefore able to undertake all things, and it completes many things, and warrants them to take effect, where he who does not love would faint and lie down." Thomas Kempis

1900: The Pouter Pigeon

After the 1860s dramatic changes in fashion could usually be noted to occur in five year cycles up until the twentieth century. At the turn of the nineteenth to twentieth century improvements in printing, clothing production, and communication reduced that cycle from five years to one year. The fashionable woman now had to update her wardrobe annually. Newly shaped corsets of the late nineteenth century completely changed a woman's posture to five it an S-bend or shape, a shape that would come to define the silhouette of the first decade of the twentieth century. This new corset had an extremely, stiff, uncomfortable front that pushed in the lower abdomen, which placed pressure on the urinary bladder, thrust the hips back, forced the chest forward, and pressed the spine into an altogether unnatural position. The effect was a forward-leaning woman with a rounded, pigeon-like bosom and an exaggerated curve to the backside. Waistlines were high at the back and drooped at the front to further exaggerate the look. Collars were stiff and high and touched the angle of the jaw to five the neck a long, lean appearance. The entire look was compared to the posture of a pouter pigeon.

During this era, now referred to as the Edwardian Era after King Edward VII who reigned from 1901 to 1910, the bosom was padded to give the effect of one enormous breast. Underskirts also rounded the backside to give the impression of one large buttock rather than two.

Small feet were so envied by women of this era that many, both men and women alike, squeezed their feet into shoes a full size smaller that their own; some even had their small toes amputated to attain the appearance of narrow feet.

By 1906 the pouter pigeon look was beginning to wand and the S-bend silhouette gave way to a straighter, more natural silhouette. The Art Nouveau movement favored flowing elegance and skirts assumed a graceful, fluid, sinuous bell shape. Bridal gowns had trained, floor length, flared skirts, tight bodices, and low necklines filled in with chemisettes of lace; the high stand collar remained popular with brides. Silk, fine cottons, linen, batiste and Swiss dot fabrics in cream, ecru and white were most popular with brides. Long, floor-length to cathedral-length diaphanous veils of sheer silk tulle fastened by crowns of wax orange buds and blossoms continued to be customary headwear for brides. Large, ornately plumed hats or a simple panache of ostrich often replaced the traditional veiling. Bridal ensembles were completed by pointed-toe shoes or boots with Louis heels, long gloves, lace or plumed fans, and even parasols.

The slipper satin gown from the 1930s depicted on the previous page has a waistline of 18 inches with forty-eight satin-covered buttons down the back and twelve satin-covered buttons on each sleeve. The trained-gown utilizes approximately twelve to fourteen yards of material and has a hemline of about one-hundred-eighty inches.

Flower Girls

Flower girls, popular in ancient Greece and Rome, fell in and out of favor many times throughout the history of marriage; the late Victorian era saw a return of their popularity. The ancient Greek and Roman flower girls scattered herbs such as rosemary, chives and garlic as symbols of fertility, while flower girls during medieval times carried and scattered sheaves of wheat for the same reason. As you look at the sweet face of this young attendant, wearing a knee-length dress puffed out by crinolines it is difficult to imagine that she would be well over 100 years old today. Young boys were often included in the wedding party as pages and aided the bride with the often-massive trains and veiling they wore during the ceremony. During the early 20th Century enormous trains began to lose favor and without a train to bear these young pages evolved into ring bearers.

This bride wears a painstakingly knife-pleated underskirt that ends in a train, as can be seen in additional photographs not included herein. Her floor-length veil is gathered at the top of her head in a tulle bow and accented with roses and an aigrette. Pale roses (*pure love, romance*), stephanotis (*married bliss*), and fern (*wisdom, fascination*) are included in her bouquet, and wax orange blossoms decorate the vamp of her silk wedding slippers.

It is unlikely that this bride, once married, worked outside of the home. In 1900 forty percent of black women and twenty percent of white women were employed in paying jobs outside of the home.

Crepe paper, cloth, and pipe cleaner cake topper circa 1918 to 1920. During the mid- to late-nineteenth century cake toppers consisted of real or confection flowers, bells, or cherubs of either confection or plaster. It wasn't until after WWI that the more commonly recognized bride and groom cake toppers almost completely replaced cake toppers of all types; they were made of paper, celluloid, plaster, bisque and plastic. Arches and bells were later additions.

Honeymoon

The honeymoon has its roots in ancient Anglo Saxon times when a bride and groom would celebrate their marriage by drinking a sweet alcoholic beverage which was made by fermenting water and honey (mead) for a period lasting for the entire phase of the moon. In cases where the bride had been captured the groom would take the bride away to some undisclosed site for a month or so, which would give the bride time to warm up to her new groom and time for her family to cool down.

The bride and bridesmaid in this turn of the century photograph are wearing matching gowns with only the veil distinguishing the bride from her attendant. The bodice is horizontally tucked, gathered, and elegantly bloused, which gives it a loose fitting appearance despite the boned and tight-fitting corset beneath. The full, gored, flared skirt is shirred at the hip and falls in expansive vertical folds to floor-length.

The maid of honor wears a large bow in her hair at the nape of the neck and pale roses to the side of her large pompadour hairstyle. Both women wear gloves, tiny corsages of pale roses, and carry presentation bouquets of fern and pale roses.

Sati ("good woman" or "chaste wife"), or suttee as it is also known, was an ancient Hindu practice in which a woman upon becoming a widow would commit suicide. The most common form of sati occurred when a woman threw herself, or was forcibly thrown, onto her dead husband's funeral pyre and so be burned to death. The practice was outlawed in 1829 although this did not entirely abolish the ritual.

Sewing the Gown

Until fairly recent times the bride often designed and even cut the pattern for her own bridal gown, but it was considered very bad luck for her to do the actual sewing. People believed that for every stitch a bride put in her wedding gown she would cry a tear during her married life. Others deemed it good luck for the last few stitches to be sewn just before leaving for, or entering, the church. It was considered bad luck if anyone sewing the gown pricked themselves and the gown became stained with blood. Good advice would be to stay away from needles altogether (as if you actually know how to sew).

Because there were no hard rules governing bridal wear it is often difficult in the absence of veils and bouquets to determine if a photograph is a wedding photograph or simply a formal photograph taken on a special occasion. The woman in this photo is a bride.

The simple, elegant, and stunning heavy duchesse satin gown has a surplice bodice trimmed in pearls and crystal beads. The satin sleeves are diagonally tucked to above elbow length and from elbow to wrist are made of the same sheer, finely dotted fabric as the yoke. The surplice bodice is continuous with the three-quarter-length V-shaped overskirt that wraps around to fasten at the left by a large satin flower. The floor length underskirt has a chapel-length pleated train. The bride wears white gloves, a brooch, and a locket and displays a flawless pompadour.

Note the wrinkles and fold marks seen in both the over- and underskirts; cutting, pinning, sewing, and ironing a gown of this quality was a monumental task in 1901 when everything was still done by hand.

"There is only one happiness in life, to love and be loved." George Sand (1804 – 1876)

The Kiss

The kiss actually symbolizes more than just a sign of endearment. In early Roman times any legal bond or contract, regardless of the gender of those entering into a contract, was "sealed with a kiss." It was also believed that the kiss was a means by which to exchange a part of each other, a method by which one person could transfer a part of themselves into the other's soul, and a way for their spirit to dwell in their spouse for all time.

While the newly married couple of today may kiss as a sign of their love, it also represents their agreement to enter into a life-long, binding contract with each other.

It is interesting to note that there is little to distinguish this turn-of-the-century bride from her attendants apart from the veil and massive beribboned bouquet of white lilies (purity, sweetness, and innocence). The dresses these women wear are so similar that any one might serve as a wedding gown.

The bride wears a gown with a fine, lace net yoke and stand-up collar. The bodice is of sheer lawn with delicate panels of lace that extend from the shoulder, where they form caps, to the waist where they are gathered by a wide sash. The same fine, diaphanous lawn forms gathered elbow-length sleeves.

The heavy satin duchesse skirt forms a chapel-length train and is open at the front to reveal a similar satin underskirt. Her tulle veil is fastened at the front of her head by a narrow band of wax orange buds and blossoms. Note the marabou trim on the dress of the bridesmaid to the extreme right. She also wears a wide headband with elaborate pearl tassels and panache of ostrich feathers.

Note the bracelets on the bride and her attendants worn at the mid-forearm; a fashion whose popularity lasted from the late Victorian era to the 1920s.

"One word frees us of all the weight and pain of life; that word is love."
Sophocles (496 – 406 B.C.)

The Threshold: bad luck or bad backs.

Belief in the power of evil, and in evil spirits, historically thought to originate in women, and to affect women more than men, is the root of many wedding customs that are still practiced today. Being carried over the threshold insured that no bride would enter her new home left foot first, or trip while entering – both prophetic of bad luck. Brides were considered especially susceptible to these demons. It was also widely believed that no evil spirit, waiting to wreak havoc on the new couple, could follow a bride into her home if she were carried through the doorway. The doorway, according to the ancient Romans, was a place where evil spirits usually lurked.

Another explanation as to why a bride is carried over the threshold is symbolic of the times when a bride was generally captured by a groom and taken by force to his home. Today that would be called abduction, a crime punishable by a long prison term. It is therefore more prudent and considerate to propose on one knee like a gentleman.

One hopes that the flowers strewn about this bride's feet are an auspicious sign for the new life she began here in 1902. Her dress of fine silk crepe is embellished with a fancy embroidered design and sheer, finely embroidered Batiste forms the bertha and flare cuffs. About midway down the skirt there is a wide row of ruching and four rows of shirring from where the lower half of the skirt flares out.

This bride wears a wide, V-shaped belt, a corsage of orange buds, and cubitals of sheer net and Batiste. The veil and blusher are gathered atop her head in high, full folds that are encircled by a crown of white roses; although the gown is not trained, the veil is chapel-length.

Cubitals are sleeves that begin above the elbow and extend to the knuckles of the hand, leaving the fingers exposed; they are not attached to the body of a dress. The name is derived from the Latin word "cubito", which means "elbow".

Because I Said So! (Who's the Boss?)

There were many superstitious practices utilized in order to determine which partner would be dominant in the new relationship, and several ways said to ensure that one would be the head of the household. The first partner over the threshold in the new home or the one who made the first purchase after the ceremony was thought to gain the upper hand. Many brides arranged to "buy" a token of some kind from a bridesmaid shortly after the vows were taken. Other brides were advised to step on their groom's foot during the vows or their first married dance or to help the groom during the ceremony when he placed the ring on her finger – this was thought to guarantee complete dominance, or at least equality. It was also held that when the bridal couple clasps hands during the vow, whoever had their thumb on top of the other's thumb would be dominant. Another method of acquiring dominance, or at least equality, was to be the first to have something to drink after the ceremony (some say it is actually the first one to take a drink in the new home, the beverage could be anything, but water seems to be the most powerful), or for the groom to kneel on part of the bridal gown during the ceremony or the bride to kneel on part of the groom's trouser. A wise bride might try all these methods – could it hurt?

This bride's unique headdress of gathered tulle draped in garlands of myrtle (*home, love, mirth, joy*) continues to draw your eye despite the opulence of the trompe l'oeil backdrop. She wears a ribbon-decorated, bloused, silk bodice with a smooth yoke and a high, sheer, stand-up, pearl-decorated collar. A chatelaine is tucked into the wide girdle at the waist. Her skirt is veiled in silk chiffon with three horizontal tucks at knee level; it flares out to the floor and has a chapel-length train.

This confident looking bride did not remove her eyeglasses for the photograph; a practice seen quite regularly in wedding photos from this period. In addition to the unique garland of the headdress, she carries a small bouquet of mountain laurel (*victory, achievement*). The total lack of intimacy, or even close association between bride and groom seen in this photograph from 1903 is something this bride's daughters would deem old fashioned.

It's Time You Took a Bride, Son.

During the late 19th Century and early 20th Century the age for men at marriage ran the gamut from very young to near middle age. It was quite common for men to wait until they were in their mid-thirties before they married. Many men as well as their practical prospective fathers-in-law believed they should be financially stable before beginning a family.

In place of the traditional bridal veil this beautiful bride chose a tulle-veiled, wide-brimmed pancake hat with a curled brim trimmed in orange blossoms. The extremely shallow crown of the hat makes the hat appear as if it sits flat on the top of her head; the tulle blusher is folded back over the top.

A lace-covered stand-up collar crowns the bodice that is bloused and gathered at the waist. She wears a deep, lace, V-shaped bertha that covers the upper arms and extends almost to the waist. The yoke is of alternating large pleats and panels of lace with the same lace insertions seen in the long, loose-fitted sleeves at points above and below the elbow.

Despite its beauty, the simple gown is completely upstaged by the choice of headwear seen in this captivating photograph of a very young couple from 1903.

A bertha is a deep trimming or collar, usually of lace, worn about the shoulders. It covers the shoulders, upper back, and breast and can extend as deep as the waist in the center.

"The average man is more interested in a woman who is interested in him than he is in a woman with beautiful legs." Marlene Dietrich (1901 – 1992)

 Helen was married in 1904 wearing a style popular at the Turn of the Century and throughout the first decade of the 20th Century. This style altered the appearance of the body to give it an S-shape, or pouter pigeon look. The curve of the bust and buttocks were exaggerated without their natural shape actually being seen. Lower cut corsets still cinched the waist but gave the bosom, backside, and hips a smooth, full appearance, a look further enhanced by blousing.

This bloused bodice has a sheer, high-necked yoke of fine Batiste embroidered with roses, and edged by three rows of tucked satin. The three-quarter length sleeves are shirred below the elbows and have wide handkerchief point lace cuffs. Tucking and ruching embellish the embroidered, V-shaped, forward sloping belt that gives the illusion of a forward drooping waistline – a look women today strive to avoid. The rounded, smooth hips have a high-riding band of shirring that further delineates the waist.

A centrally inserted panel of the same sheer, rose-embroidered Batiste decorates the front of the skirt from waist to floor. She wears white gloves, a locket, and displays a flawless Gibson girl pompadour under a finely shirred silk wedding crown.

The Bride Feeds the Groom

The practice of the bride and groom each feeding the other a piece of the wedding cake is an old and very beautiful custom which symbolizes their desire to nurture and provide for each other throughout their life together. If, while feeding each other, a bit of icing daubs the lips or face it portends a rich, sweet life together, but if icing is smeared on the face, especially purposely, it foretells of a troubled marriage. Unfortunately, this custom has become a joke at many weddings as the cake is often smeared on the face of an unwary bride or groom; this hopefully is not symbolic of the way each means to treat the other in future.

The origin of feeding cake to each other goes back to the ancient Romans and their rigid codes of marriage. The most common form of marriage, practiced by the lower classes, was "usus" in which a woman lived with a man for a period of one year after which she was considered his wife. They could choose to solemnize this arrangement or continue as they were – providing the woman spent three consecutive nights of each year away from the man. Either party could dissolve this type of marriage at any time.

A second type of marriage was known as "coemptio" in which a wife was purchased in front of at least five male witnesses.

"Confarrentio" is the method from which feeding of the cake is derived. It was a ceremony performed only between members of the elite patrician class of Romans. The ceremony had to be solemnized by the high priest of Rome and took place before ten male witnesses; this was considered a marriage for life. The marriage contract was sealed when the bride and groom shared a wheat cake. This was a very difficult marriage to dissolve.

An old custom that many brides still practice today is to save a piece of the wedding cake (usually the top layer or tier) for the couple's first anniversary or the baptism celebration of their first child.

The rich tones seen in this high quality photograph, circa 1904, enable the viewer to note and appreciate the elaborate detailing in this gown of fine lawn. It should also be noted that as the Victorian era drew to a close wedding poses became more intimate, even affectionate in nature.

A yoke of lace sets off a pleated, gathered, bloused, lace bodice. Below-the-elbow sleeves have lace chevron inserts and end in wide, bell-shaped, lace-frilled cuffs tied with a bow. The bride's skirt is decorated at the knee and hem with horizontal tucks and bands of lace.

Her embroidered net veil is gathered at the crown and held atop her rolled hair by wax orange blossoms and silk lily of the valley (*return of happiness*). She wears long, sheer gloves with lace insertions, and carries a waterfall bouquet of light and dark zinnias (*fond memory, lasting affection*), fern (*fascination*), and angel vine (*intoxication*).

I've Never Seen a Yellow Bride

It was a widely held belief that if you married in blue your love would always be true. The Chinese, however, consider red to be the color of luck: the bride wears red, the bridal decorations are red, monetary gifts are given in red envelopes and a red umbrella often shades the bride during the ceremony. Early Celtic women also considered red to be a lucky color and were married wearing red gowns, although today, among Westerners red is considered a hard luck color for a wedding gown as noted by this popular rhyme:

Married in gray, you'll go far away. Married in black, you'll wish yourself back. Married in brown, you'll live out of town. Married in red, you'll wish yourself dead. Married in pearl, you'll live in a whirl. Married in green, ashamed to be seen. Married in yellow, jealous of your fellow. Married in blue, he'll always be true. Married in pink, your spirits will sink. Married in white, everything's right. Some cultures believe a woman who wears a yellow bridal dress is apt to cheat.

Oops, Must be Those Demons

Any mishap during the wedding ceremony is generally considered to portend bad luck, even if the reason behind the superstition is not known. It would surprise most people to learn that one mishap, dropping the ring, considered bad luck today was originally considered a favorable omen. Because all the evil spirits would be shaken out of it when it hit the ground, many of our ancestors considered it a good omen if the groom dropped the wedding ring during the ceremony. Rather than bad luck, it is more likely the sweaty, trembling hands and stress associated with a wedding that cause rings to be dropped.

Ostrich plumes decorate this expertly balanced, rather large, wide-brimmed hat that appears perched atop this bride's head. Her elaborate gown has fancy frill-edges and a guipure lace bertha with a high, stand-up, ruff collar embellished by lace, embroidery, frills and a large pearl drop necklace.

The bloused bodice is of Swiss dot and has large three-quarter length puff sleeves decorated with floral cuffs, bands of lace, satin inserts and dotted Swiss; the sleeves end in faux under sleeves. She wears long white gloves with buttons. A sheer overskirt of dotted Swiss with lace trim and a double-tucked hem of satin veils a satin underskirt that is accordion pleated at the bottom. Her bouquet contains more than three-dozen pale roses; quite an armful for even the strongest bride.

Trompe l'oeil studio backdrops have been a component of photographs since the earliest days of photography; they, like this one from 1905, became larger with time and, as a result of electricity and elaborate lighting, more three-dimensional.

The Garter Toss: Here You Go Boys

The Garter Toss is one of the oldest surviving wedding traditions. During ancient times it was customary for friends, relatives, and guests to accompany the bridal couple to the marriage bed. The families of the newlyweds, and many guests, clamored for articles of the bride's clothing, which were considered to be lucky charms. Many guests often remained to witness the consummation of the marriage and test the veracity of the bride's virginity and thus justify the amount paid to her family. Nothing less than blood satisfied these onlookers, and goodness help the bride who didn't provide the proper amount. In Medieval times a piece of the bride's gown was considered a good luck charm and guests would snatch pieces off the garment. This event became quite rowdy to the point that some guests were all too eager to help the bride out of her wedding clothes, often leaving her completely undressed. To forestall such impropriety, the garters were quickly removed, often immediately after the ceremony, and, along with the bouquet, thrown to the mob as a distraction that allowed the couple to get away unscathed. As time went on it has evolved into the tradition we practice today and signifies marriage for the single man who catches it.

Blue is the chosen color of the garter based on the blue velvet garter worn below the left knee on Queens and princesses, and what is a woman on the day of her wedding if not a queen?

This bride wears a white gown of fine lawn and batiste that has a bloused bodice and bishop sleeves both with lace insertions. Wide, bell-shaped, batiste cuffs, very popular in 1905, trim the tight cuffs of the voluminous bishop sleeves; many rows of lace insertions embellish the flare skirt. The high rolled-collar and large, V-shaped bertha are of fine, figured Batiste. She wears a locket and a simple bar-pin on the collar.
Her mature groom may have been one of the more prudent, practical men who achieved financial security prior to matrimonial bliss.

Wine + Wine = One

The French have a lovely custom that anyone may utilize at their own wedding. To signify their newly created alliance and the uniting of two as one they each take a glass of wine from two different vineyards, pour the wine from those glasses into a third glass and then drink of this newly mixed wine.

The bride in this striking 1906 photograph embodies the classic Gibson girl with the easily identifiable pouter-pigeon figure. The tiny, corseted waist is made to appear even smaller by the puffed bodice, huge double-puff sleeves, smooth well-defined hip and flare skirt. This gown of rich duchesse satin with a chapel-length train is gathered at the waist and falls in full, wide folds to the floor. The skirt is embellished by a tucked chou of lace with two lace panels fastened by an agraffe of wax orange blossoms. Around the bottom of the skirt there are large butterfly-shaped lace inserts.

Her veil and blusher of silk illusion tulle is attached to her rolled pompadour by a crown of wax orange blossoms; a star-shaped pearl pin secures a knotted lace jabot.

The plain, contrasting dark background in this photograph offers no distractions from this spectacular bride – something to consider when having your own photographs taken.

*"A successful marriage requires falling in love many times,
always with the same person."* Mingnon McLaughlin

Bride on the Left

As a result of the early practice of gaining a bride by capture, brides traditionally stand to the left of their grooms. Many early Anglo Saxon grooms needed a free sword hand to prevent the abduction of his bride from a former suitor, or defend his prize from the bride's family during the ceremony. It was important for his right hand, his sword hand, to be free. An added measure of protection was to enlist the aide of his best friend, or best man, to watch his back, so to speak, during the parts of the ceremony when he might be distracted. Thankfully the reason for this positioning has long gone the way of the Round Table; today's grooms have enough problems with studs, cufflinks, ties, and cummerbunds.

This fine, fancy dress of sheer, embroidered Batiste and silk organdy, circa 1907, is rivaled for attention by the bride's large, unusual hat. The under-brim of the heart-shaped hat is of shirred organza on a wire frame edged in deep ruching. The hat is garnished above and below by a garland of wax orange buds and blossoms and tied under the chin with a wide ribbon. She has the high pompadour hairstyle popular at the turn-of-the-century and wears pince-nez, gloves and a watch around her neck.

In many cultures men are expected to marry or face dire consequences. Fijians believed a man would turn to ashes and be banned from paradise if he died a bachelor. In Siberia it was considered heresy for a man not to marry, and a man who dies a bachelor is doomed to haunt the earth.

The bride with the far-away expression wears a gown with a bloused high-necked bodice that falls in deep folds over a silk sash belt ending in two large tassels. The slightly trained skirt has a shirred hip yoke, shirring at shin level, and ends in three narrow horizontal tucks. Her wide sleeves are shirred at the top.

Tin Cans, Honking Horns, and Old Shoes

When the drivers in a bridal procession honk their horns, or motorists beep their car horns upon seeing a bridal party they are taking part in the very ancient and cross-cultural tradition of scaring away evil spirits who are said to be sensitive to, and repelled by, loud noises. This is also the reason people used to tie tin cans to the back of a newly wedded couple's vehicle.

Leather was considered protection against evil spirits and old shoes, forms of barter and symbols of good luck since ancient times were often tossed at the bridal couple's carriage. Good luck to the couple was ensured for every shoe that hit their vehicle, and extremely good luck for each shoe that landed on the carriage's roof. Later on old shoes were tied to the vehicle as wishes for good luck. In ancient times shoes were considered a symbol of wealth and prosperity as only those of the upper classes could afford shoes; slaves in ancient Greece and Rome went barefoot.

"There is nothing nobler or more admirable then when two people who see eye to eye keep house as man and wife, confounding their enemies and delighting their friends." Homer *The Odyssey (800 B. C.)*

1910: The Waist is Emancipated and Hemlines Rise

The second decade of the twentieth century heralded a new freedom for women both in society and fashion. The women's suffrage movement was strong and gaining momentum. World War One began in 1914, though the U.S.A. did not enter the battle until 1917, resulting in women taking on occupations outside the home. Restrictive, uncomfortable corsets and cumbersome underskirts became relics of the past. One interesting and incredibly restrictive style seen early in the decade was the hobble skirt, so called because the skirt was so tight at the ankle women literally had to hobble. Their stride was limited to a couple of inches – any stride longer than that would risk a fall or tear in the dress. It is difficult to imagine women embracing such a style after rejecting the corsets and heavy undergarments worn only a few years earlier. Many women went so far as to bind their ankles together with a short length of rope in order to keep their steps short and skirts intact. Brides were not exempt from the folly of wearing the peculiar and short-lived fashion.

Looser, more comfortable clothing of rich, lighter weight, delicate materials became the mode for casual, formal, and bridal wear. Skirts were puffy or bouffant and hemlines rose to mid-calf by 1915. Women began to wear make-up and wore simple jewelry or no jewelry at all; brides routinely began to wear pearls. Hairstyles were sleek, smooth, and neatly arranged with emphasis at the sides rather than the top and for the first time women parted their hair on the side.

As hemlines rose, necklines lowered in a variety of shapes that exposed the neck, throat, and collar bones – body parts long considered provocative, even erotic. Square, boat-shaped, and round necklines were most in vogue, while sleeves were long, fitted, dolman, raglan, or three-quarter length. Ecru, ivory, cream and white in fabrics such as silk, silk jersey, batiste, crepe-de-chine, or silk georgette (plain, embroidered, or beaded)) continued as the most popular colors and materials for wedding gowns. Bridal fashions changed rapidly during this decade and embraced every aspect of the newer designs. A mass of tulle, chiffon, and other gauzy materials were applied to give gowns a light, ethereal charm. Many brides chose shorter veils of net, tulle, or lace to complement the shorter gowns. Elbow-length, finger-tip, and waltz (ballet) length veils became very fashionable, although sweep, chapel, and cathedral-lengths were worn as often as not with the newer shorter gowns. Enormous, bandeau-bound bridal crowns were favored by the end of the decade, although large hats with wide brims maintained their popularity if not with the bride then certainly with the bridesmaids. Silk stockings and silk or brocade shoes with decorative, cross-over bar straps, Louis heels, cutwork vamps, and pointed toes were, by this time de rigueur for brides. Monumental bouquets with massive ribbons were the trend. Bandeaus, a glamorous name for a fancy headband, became increasingly popular after 1900. Bandeaus were made of any type of material with satin being the favorite. They were simple, embroidered, shirred, had ruching, pleats or jewels and fastened veils or plumes to the head. The bandeau attained its fashion zenith during the 1920s and could be easily made to complement any dress or gown.

Sawhorsing

In Italy during the 19ᵗʰ and early 20ᵗʰ Centuries there was a practice known as "sawhorsing" which symbolized the partnership of a newly married couple and the importance of working together as a team to build a future together. A log was set up on a pair of sawhorses and the newly married couple, with the encouragement of family and friends and the aid of a two-man saw, cut the log in two. It was also customary for the Italian groom to carry a piece of iron in his pocket as protection against "malocchio", the evil eye.

An extremely high, ruched, stand up collar, a large, fancy lace bertha, and a lace trimmed, inverted-V cut overskirt with a wide sash belt give this 1912 bride a long, narrow look. An ankle-length, silk taffeta underskirt with a train completes the ensemble and adds a touch of elegance. The chapel-length veil is gathered in pleats atop the bride's head and decorated with a fringe of lily of the valley (*return of happiness*). She carries a large waterfall bouquet of lilies (*sweetness, wealth, gaiety*) with bits of fern (*fascination*) knotted in the long, trailing satin streamers; she wears white gloves and a pince-nez.

Physical contact between a bride and her groom, even if it is just a hand resting on a shoulder, is seen in photographs with much more frequency as the first decade of the 20ᵗʰ Century comes to a close.

By the time this bride was married: women in New Mexico (1910) had won partial suffrage, women in Washington (1910) and California (1911) had full suffrage, and in 1912 women in Arizona, Kansas, and Oregon were granted full suffrage.

"Only choose in marriage a man whom you would choose as a friend if he were a woman." Joseph Joubert (1754 – 1824)

The bride's crepe silk bodice is almost completely hidden by her large bouquet of fern and white roses with its broad, figured batiste bow and trailing ribbons. The bodice has a scoop neckline, short sleeves, and a natural waist. The silk chiffon skirt, gathered beneath a wide sash, is smooth and simple from the waist to the lower thigh at which point it is decorated by rows of wide, draping frills. A crown of white roses holds her long, sheer tulle veil, which adds an ethereal tone to the image.

Her presentation bouquet of white roses (*love, worthiness*) and asparagus fern (*sincerity*) is tied with a broad, figured Batiste bow that covers the front of the bride's skirt. She wears no jewelry around her neck; however, a very large engagement ring and wedding band are clearly visible on her left-hand ring finger.

While brides of her generation had a say in what man they would marry, they still had no say in who was to be the president of their own country. In 1913 women in Illinois won partial suffrage, women in Alaska won full suffrage, and a year later, women in Nevada and Montana gained full suffrage. By the time this woman married, a number of states had limited voting rights for women, a right still denied to women in most of the country yet a right offered to all men, even the uneducated, illiterate, and immigrant.

Trying on the Ring

It is generally thought to be bad luck to let another person try on your engagement ring, however, in parts of Scotland when a woman becomes engaged her friends may try her ring on their engagement finger up to the middle knuckle only, never all the way. They turn the ring three times toward their heart and make a silent wish that is supposed to come true. In some cultures it is considered lucky to make a wish on the bride's engagement ring.

"Love takes off masks that we fear we cannot live without and know
we cannot live within." James A. Baldwin (1924 – 1987)

Gloves

Suitors of old would send a pair of gloves to the woman who aroused their passion and if she wore the gloves to Sunday Mass it meant she returned the sentiment. Greek brides tuck a lump of sugar in their wedding gloves to guarantee a married life filled with sweetness, and salt, long believed to have protective benefits against witches and wicked spirits, was sprinkled in the gloves of many Northern European brides.

A Gainsborough painting might well have been the inspiration for the splendid gown worn by this bride in 1915. The gown is opulent without being garish and the rich, luxurious materials of lace, tulle, and shimmering satin give this woman a stunning, vibrant effect. A variation of the hoopskirt returned briefly about this time, albeit smaller and not as cumbersome. The shape of this gown was maintained by two lightweight hoops; one at the level of the knee and one at mid-calf. French knots along the hem of the satin overskirt fasten a deep panel of lace veiling below the knee that has wire sewn in the hem enabling it to be shaped into the cascading form seen here. Fine detail can be appreciated on this gown from the delicate ruff neckline of the tulle bodice to the rows of tiny tucks seen at the hem. A small portion of the court train may be seen extending from the left shoulder.

Her large silk hat is swathed in yards of tulle and adorned with silk posies to complete an altogether elegant, captivating appearance. She wears a gold bangle at mid-forearm.

"Women wish to be loved without a why or a wherefore; not because they are pretty, or good, or well bred, or graceful, or intelligent, but because they are themselves."
Henri Frederic Amiel (1821 – 1881)

In 1916 this modern bride chose a less formal dress for her wedding ceremony. The unusual satin bodice is gathered and bloused as was typical for the time. The low scoop neckline and bare shoulders, however, could only have been worn during a civil ceremony and never in a church unless worn with a chemise or wrapper.

The smooth satin skirt has short, puffed panniers, and a fine net shawl veils her arms and gives the dress a light, blithe charm. She wears no jewelry - a short-lived fashion of the time.

During this same year a feminist named Alice Paul together with other women picketed the White House in an attempt to pressure President Wilson to support passage of a constitutional amendment that would permit women their right to vote in national elections. They shocked the nation and world by chaining themselves to the White House fence. The year 1916 also saw the first female member of Congress, Jeannette Rankin, from Montana, who was elected to the House of Representatives.

Diamonds, Symbols of Eternal Love: Invincible, Eternal & Unchanging

Diamonds have long held an attraction for men. It was believed by the ancient Greeks that diamonds were the teardrops of the gods and they contained the fires of love. In fact, the word diamond is a derivative of the Greek word "adamas" meaning: invincible, eternal and unchanging. Ancient Romans thought them to be fragments of the stars that were used as arrow tips by the god of love, Eros – quite a romantic notion. Thus the power of love was a force both cultures attributed to the diamond.

The diamond engagement ring originated during the 15th Century when King Maximilian of Austria presented Mary of Burgundy with a diamond ring as a token of his love. They were married in 1477. During the 16th Century the Venetians popularized this practice and a tradition was born.

Engagement rings were worn on the little-used fourth finger of the least dominant hand, the left in most women, in order to prevent damage to the ring during the performance of everyday tasks in a right hand dominant society. In addition to this practical approach the ancient Egyptians, and subsequently the Romans, believed that the fourth finger on the left hand contained a blood vessel "vena amoris" that went directly to the heart, the organ long considered the seat of love.

Today, over three billion dollars a year is spent on diamond engagement rings.

The Eternal Circle

Many brides chose a headdress of a simple circlet of orange buds and blossoms, or a wreath of flowers simply because they preferred the look. The circular headdress has roots that date to a time earlier than the cultures of the ancient Greeks and Romans. Superstition tells us that no evil spirit may enter a circle and so, aside from its symbolism for eternity, a circle anywhere on or around the body afforded extra protection from the all too ubiquitous phantoms whose antics and malevolence prove to be the root of many of our "modern" wedding practices.

A large circlet of wax orange buds and blossoms fastens the net-cap headpiece that was extremely popular during the 1910s to the early 1920s. The headpiece on this bride from 1916 sits low on the forehead and ears, exactly in the manner in which it was meant to be worn. The bride wears a silk chiffon gown with an unusual dentate collar, and carries a large presentation bouquet of white roses with a wide, satin-edged, tulle bow.

Her attendant wears a lovely, silk, wide-brimmed hat with a deep frill and a posy at the crown.

"Remember if you marry for beauty, thou bindest thyself all thy life for that which perchance, will neither last nor please thee one year: and when thou hast it, it will be to thee of no price at all." Emily Dickinson (1830 – 1886)

Breaking Bread over the Bride's Head

Another old custom that was practiced to ensure happiness and fertility is for the mother-in-law of the bride to break a loaf of bread above the bride's head as the bride enters her new home. It's not a custom one would recommend practicing or adopting if the bride's relationship with her in-laws is less than perfect, and the bread less than fresh. And remember, the bread is broken in half or crumbled *above* the bride's head – she is not actually clobbered.

The bride's belted, ankle-length, silk georgette gown is heavily beaded in crystal and pearls from bodice to hem. She wears white silk shoes, white gloves, and a wedding ring over the gloved finger. Her silk floral crown fastens a chapel-length tulle veil, and the bouquet of pale carnations is tied with a broad ribbon of tulle edged in narrow bands of satin.

The maid of honor wears a heavily beaded, silk georgette, chiffon-veiled dress with handkerchief points. Her headdress is nothing more than shirred tulle gathered by a satin bandeau, quite chic in 1916, and she wears a ring over tightly fitted, silk, elbow-length gloves.

Note the relaxed, even casual, pose assumed by the bride - unremarkable by today's standards but slightly progressive for women of her generation.

"The ultimate test of a relationship is to disagree but hold hands." Alexander Penney

Tulle

The material known as tulle has its origins in early 19th Century France (1818) and is named for the town, Tulle, which began producing the soft, sheer material on wide looms. This gossamer material has the ability to soften the lines of any clothing and gives any look an ethereal charm. The exotic, even erotic, tulle blusher not only adds a touch of mystery and beauty to a bride, it also provides a very tender and romanticized moment when it is lifted by the bride's father for the kiss with which he gives her away or lifted by the groom for the couple's first kiss as man and wife.

In 1917, this bride carried a large, beribboned bouquet of baby's breath (*modesty, sweet beauty*) and more than two-dozen pale roses (*pink for romance and tender feelings, white for pure love*). Her simple ankle-length gown of chiffon has a low, V-cut neckline and short, flare, slit sleeves.

The headpiece on this bride is the true eye-catcher. This shirred tulle bandeau heavily ornamented with wax orange blossoms and buds fastens a cathedral-length tulle veil with a high, stiffened tulle corona. Her pointy, waist-heel, t-strap shoes button at the instep and have cutout crossover detail and a cutout design on the vamp. She wears formal length gloves gathered above the elbow and a long string of pearls.

In 1917 12,000 women were hired by the U. S. Navy to fill jobs vacated by men who were being sent overseas. They were hired at the same wage and classification as the men who filled the jobs before them. In the same year, women in New York won full suffrage, while women in Arkansas, Indiana, Rhode Island, Nebraska, and North Dakota won partial suffrage; women in Indiana lost that right before the year was out, but fought and won it back in 1919.

Bouquets or Boo-quets

Few brides today would imagine that the bouquets they carry is a practice rooted in ancient superstition, nor would they recognize the bouquets carried by their early sisters. Brides originally carried bouquets of herbs and spices. It was thought that the more potent the odor of the bouquet, the more protective it would be for the bride; strong smelling herbs and spices were believed to drive off evil spirits and the threat of ill luck and poor health. Bouquets of garlic, onion, and chives were among those favored for the walk down the aisle. One could imagine an ancient bride adding her bouquet to the couple's first home cooked meal as they often did. The Romans later included flowers to symbolize new life, fertility, and beauty; the flowers eventually won out.

This bride literally takes the bridal headdress to new heights, and one may well joke that she could travel to her honeymoon destination with aid of nothing more than a good strong headwind. The waltz-length tulle veil, which sits low on the brow and completely covers her head, is gathered and fastened by a narrow bandeau of wax orange buds and blossoms into an expansive, radiant corona.

A sheer, crystal-beaded tunic veils her shin-length, silk underdress. She wears a string of pearls, a lavaliere with a pearl drop and white silk crossover strap shoes with high heels. Her beribboned bouquet is of white roses, fern and lily of the valley.

"The love we have in our youth is superficial compared to the love that an old man has for his old wife." Will Durant (1885 – 1981). This quote from Will Durant, an American writer, historian and philosopher, proved more true than sentimental. At the age of 96 Will Durant was seriously ill and hospitalized. Ariel, his wife, became so stressed about Will's health that she could no longer eat and as a result she died a few days before their 68th wedding anniversary. Upon learning of his wife's death, Will died as well.

Brides During War

During periods of war, brides often chose to be married wearing their best dress in place of the traditional white bridal costume. Aside from the scarcity of goods, which occurred as a result of war, many brides felt that the somber times required simple weddings. Brides curtailed elaborate celebrations in the absence of their fathers and brothers who might have been enlisted overseas, while other brides were hastily married before their fiancés went off to war. Sadly, somber weddings were also the weddings of choice for those brides mourning the loss of family members killed in action.

This 1917 bride wears a simple, elegant, non-traditional wedding outfit. A very high seal skin collar tops a dark coat, which is decorated with a latticed, hand-knotted, extremely wide fringe. Her only indulgence in terms of bridal accessories is the heavily beribboned bouquet of fern and roses and a bit of lace veiling on her hat.

Proxy Bouquet

The Victorians were especially noted for their specialty bouquets. They would incorporate all types of symbolism in the form of flowers, leaves, herbs, charms, and even an occasional horseshoe or two. Another wonderful custom that you may easily incorporate in your wedding plans is to use the "bouquet" or "hat" made out of ribbons and bows during your bridal shower as the proxy bouquet during your wedding rehearsal. .

"Wither thou goest, I will go; and where thou lodgest, I will lodge: thy people shall be my people and thy God my God." The Bible, Ruth 1:16

Seize the Day

February 29th, a day that occurs once every four years during a leap year, was conceived of as a way to adjust the discrepancy between the time it takes for the Earth to complete one orbit of the sun (365 days and 6 hours) and the traditional calendar of 365 days. This day, actually composed of 6 hours from each of the preceding four years, was not considered a "true" day in English law, and as such held no merit and was simply ignored or leapt over. So, as tradition holds, it was on this day that St. Patrick (after much complaining by St. Bridget that prevailing custom only allowed men to propose and as a result many women were left unmarried) allowed women to adjust, in addition to the calendar, that injustice and gave them the right to propose to the unmarried man of her choice. Laws, dating back to at least the 13th Century in Scotland held that any man who refused a proposal of marriage on February 29th would be fined. In the United States, February 29th is referred to as Sadie Hawkins day after the character of the same name in Al Capp's *Lil' Abner* comic series.

This bride, married in London in 1918 during World War I chose a white satin gown veiled in embroidered silk chiffon. The satin skirt is veiled in the same embroidered silk chiffon and is gathered at the waist from where it falls in loose folds to a wide, satin, ankle-length band. The tulle cap sits low on the forehead, has a border of gathered tulle and gives off a fingertip-length veil gathered at each temple by a cluster of wax orange buds and blossoms.

Women in Michigan, Oklahoma, and South Dakota won full suffrage in 1918, while their sisters in Texas won partial suffrage.

Elaborate and fashionable are words that accurately describe the wedding party in this photo dated 1918. The bride wears a chiffon-veiled georgette dress with the low, round neckline of the chiffon veiling just a bit higher than the neckline of the georgette under- skirt. Her three-quarter length sleeves end in a wide, turned-back, boat-shaped cuff. Silver bugle beads decorate the chiffon overskirt in an overall design. Her stockings and shoes are of white silk and her fingertip-length tulle veil with elbow-length blusher is gathered atop her head by an interesting corona of silk lily of the valley. The beribboned waterfall bouquet of silk orange blossoms and fern trails silk streamers of knotted fern.

Similar, though smaller, bouquets are tucked in the bodices of her female attendants who each wear dresses of a completely different style. The attendant to the right of the bride wears a georgette dress with an empire waist, deep V-shaped neckline, elbow-length sleeves, and shin-length tiered skirt. Her stockings are white, as are her Louis-heeled silk shoes. She wears a helmet cloche cap with turned-up brim decorated by like-fabric flowers and wears elbow-length gloves.

The attendant to the bride's left wears a satin dress with an elaborate lace overskirt. The bodice has short puff sleeves gathered with silk flowers and horizontal tucks of satin across the bust and waist; it ends in a satin peplum-like ruffle. Her large-crowned, wide-brimmed hat is veiled in fine, almost transparent, lace; it has ruching on the underside of the brim and appears to be of the same silver satin as her bow-tied, Louis-heeled satin shoes. Notice her heavily textured, up-to-the-minute-fashion stockings. All three women wear the de rigueur string of pearls.

"When you fish for love, bait with your heart, not your brain."
Mark Twain (1835 – 1910)

June Bride

"Marry in May and you'll live to rue the day" is an adage based on ancient Pagan customs. The festival of Beltane, also known as May Eve, May Day, and Walpurgis Night, was observed at the beginning of the month of May. It was a festival of flowers, crops, and fertility, which was celebrated by outdoor orgies in gardens and fields (supposedly to insure the fertility of the crops) – an unsuitable time to begin married life.

May was also the month in which the Romans observed the Feast of the Dead and a festival dedicated to the goddess of chastity – also not an auspicious time to begin married life. The month of June, however, was named after Juno, the Roman goddess of love and marriage, and was therefore considered a lucky month in which to marry.

"Marry in Lent, live to repent." In the Christian Church Lent is not considered a good time to marry as Lent is typically a time of abstinence – generally not a practice well suited to a honeymoon. Some churches will allow marriage during Lent, but rarely during Holy Week (the week between Palm Sunday and Easter) and never during the Sacred Triduum: Holy Thursday, Good Friday and Easter Sunday. Christians who choose to marry during lent are encouraged to do so without much festivity.

For those who do choose to Marry in June or September, the two most popular months for weddings, the cost can run about thirty-percent more than those married in November through April. Incidentally, couples that opt to marry on Friday the thirteenth, or even the thirteenth day of the month may save up to fifty-percent on the wedding venue; something to think about.

This young bride wears a calf-length, silk chiffon dress with lace cap sleeves and bows at the shoulder. Her cathedral-length tulle veil with blusher is trimmed with a wide border of lace and is gathered in a large chou at the back of the head completely exposing the crown. It is fastened by three rows of elaborately patterned wax orange buds with a draped garland of wax orange blossoms at each ear.

She carries a large bouquet of pale roses, fern, and lily of the valley; the cascading satin ribbons of the bouquet are tied in elaborate bows.

In the year in which this bride married, 1919, partial suffrage was won by women in Indiana, Maine, Missouri, Ohio, and Tennessee.

1920: Bosoms and Bottoms Disappear

Ankle-length bridal gowns dominated the 1920s both early and late in the decade; however, the style seen from 1923 to 1928 is the fashion that has come to characterize the entire decade of the flapper bride. She was intelligent, witty, daring, independent, and sexy. She bobbed, waved, shingled, or Eton-cropped her hair. She voted, wore vibrantly colored make-up, smoked, danced outlandishly, consumed cocktails, worked, and even exposed her upper arms, shoulders and knees – the "nude" look. Her forehead, however, seldom saw the light of day. Between cloche caps, bandeaus, diadems, and headache bands a truly fashionable woman might have passed a good part of the decade with ever exposing her forehead. Cloche caps and bandeaus, though part of everyday wear were quickly adapted for the bride and bridesmaid.

Beaded dresses of silk, Georgette, crepe-de-chine, and a variety of durable, man-made materials were very popular with the flapper bride. Shapeless, elongated torsos with no hint of breasts and dropped waistlines defined the look of the 1920s. Flat chests and slim, boyish hips were attained by binding the breasts and wearing tube-shaped bodices that extended beyond the waist to the hips (the drop waist). Boat-shaped, V-shaped, low round, and scoop necklines as well as cowl collars were quite trendy for bridal gowns. Kimono sleeves were favored but raglan and dolman sleeves maintained their popularity. The newest and boldest of these new trends in wedding gowns, however, was the sleeveless gown.

The wedding gown could be straight and shapeless or flared, pleated, or bouffant. Early in the 1920s wedding gowns were ankle or calf-length but by the mid-1920s wedding hemlines were just below the knee or knee-length. After the mid-1920s bridal gowns became longer and uneven at the hem, often lower in the back than in the front. Handkerchief point hemlines became the rage. Most brides wore traditional veils and it was quite common to see a bride in a knee-length dress with an heirloom lace, cathedral-length veil dragging behind. Large, sheer, horsehair hats with drooping brims, cloche, helmet cloche, and brimless cloche caps were also considered very chic for brides and their attendants. Silk, brocade, or leather shoes with cutwork vamps and cross-over bar straps were the most preferred shoe for wedding wear.

The bride pictured on the previous page wears a satin gown with paniers, a chapel-length panel train, and a chapel-length tulle veil. She was right in style for a woman being married during the early 1920s. Not long after this bride married hemlines began to rise, reaching to just below the knee at mid-decade.

Choosing Two Men

Brides married during this year had the right to choose their own wedding gowns, their own bridesmaids, their own husbands, and for the first time in the history of the United States, their own president. Because of their heroic and active participation during The Great War (World War I) a constitutional amendment for women's suffrage was, by a narrow margin, passed by Congress in 1919. The 19th Amendment to The Constitution, which gave women the right to vote, was finally ratified in 1920. It is difficult to imagine that in 1970, fifty years after they were found competent enough to choose the president of the United States many women still required their husband's signature when applying for a mortgage or credit card.

By 1920 hemlines were well on their way up. This bride wears a calf-length, satin dress with a low V-shaped neckline, narrow satin shoulder straps, and sheer, silver beaded sleeves; the bouffant skirt is decorated with silver bugle beads. A large ostrich plume decorates her right hip; she wears long white gloves, white stockings and Louis-heeled, wide strapped, side-buttoned shoes, and a string of pearls.

Her voluminous cathedral-length tulle veil falls from a diadem-shaped crown that is studded with pearls and decorated at each side with a cluster of wax orange blossoms and pearls. A cathedral-length Watteau train falls from her shoulders and is clearly seen in the forefront of the photo.

The most precious possession that ever comes to a man in this world
is a woman's heart." J. G. Holland (1819 – 1881)

115

Confetti

The word confetti is Italian in origin and refers to a sugarcoated morsel, usually nuts or dried fruits. The ancient Romans tossed confetti in the form of honey-coated nuts and bits of dried fruits to celebrate both weddings and births.

Confetto, or sugar coated almonds, representative of the sweetness (sugar) and bitterness (almond) life has to offer can still be found at almost any Italian wedding at every place setting. They usually come in groups of five (health, wealth, long life, fertility, and happiness) and may be found in small fancy boxes or wrapped in tiny tulle bags (bomboniere). A very charming tradition is for the bride, along with her family and friends, to tie these Confetto (also known as Jordan Almonds) in tiny bags of excess tulle cut from her veil, or in tulle cut from the same bolt of tulle from which her veil was cut.

This simple georgette dress has sheer short sleeves with wide lace cuffs and a wide scoop neckline. The real eye-catcher in this photograph from 1921 is the distinctive, fancy, lace bandeau that fastens the translucent chiffon veil. The top of the bride's head is bare, revealing a waved hairstyle with a part on the side; she wears sheer, figured, elbow-length gloves. It was not until the early twentieth century that it became socially acceptable for women to part their hair on the side; prior to this, only men were permitted to do so.

Note the string of pearls is now quite long as compared with the short string of pearls worn during the previous decades

Throwing Rice

Showering a newly married couple in grains such as rice, barley, oats, wheat, or even raisins, nuts, or flowers was long believed to ensure a couple's fertility. In China, a young male child is made to play or jump on the marriage bed to not only guarantee fertility, but also to make certain that the first-born child is a male.

In Scotland, newlyweds were assured to achieve a fertile future if a woman with milk in her breasts prepared the marriage bed, and in Ireland the same outcome was almost certain if the couple spent their marriage night in a bed that had a laying hen tied to the bedpost. Today ecologically friendly bubbles, birdseed, or biodegradable confetti are substituted for grains.

This bride wears a short-sleeved, ankle-length, satin dress with a low, round neckline decorated by a thick row of tiny pearls. The duchesse satin skirt is puffed at the hips and falls to ankle-length where a fancy lace underskirt can be seen.

Her chapel-length tulle veil forms a cap that is secured by a wide crown of wax orange blossoms and is trimmed with sprays and garlands of the same. Satin, three-button, crossover strap shoes, very current in 1921, and elbow-length gloves complete the outfit. Her large, round bouquet of pale roses and fern has many cascading satin ribbons knotted with fern.

The maid of honor wears a wide bandeau, or "headache band," of satin flowers that completely covers her forehead. Her bouquet of dark roses and fern is tied with a wide, glossy ribbon fashioned into a large bow.

"There is no more lovely, friendly and charming relationship, communion or company than a good marriage." Martin Luther

Old, New, Borrowed, Blue and a Lucky Coin

A tradition many brides practiced in order to bring them luck, fortune, and protection against want was to put a sterling coin or lucky penny, in their wedding shoe or glove before the marriage ceremony. The coin was saved and often worn around the neck or on a bracelet as a memento of the bride's wedding day. Most people are familiar with, and are even able to quote the adage about "something old, something new…" but the last line is usually omitted for some unknown reason.

"Something old, something new, something borrowed, something blue, and a sixpence (*penny*) in your shoe." Something old symbolized the bride's continued connection with her family and past, something new for prosperity in the bride's future, something borrowed (from a happily married woman and which must be returned) to signify that a bride's family and friends would continue to lend support, and that some of the happy woman's luck would rub off. Blue has been the color of purity, constancy, faithfulness, and loyalty since early Biblical times. The sixpence (penny) in the shoe was believed to ensure future financial security and happiness.

Each decade had its own defining style: silk georgette, bugle beading, and long, slim, shapeless lines distinguished the look of the early to mid-1920s.

This bride wears a silk georgette under-dress with sheer, crystal-beaded veiling. The dress has a scoop neck and short handkerchief-point sleeves edged in crystal bugle beads. Her fine, satin-edged, tulle veil shimmers with medallions of crystal beading and satin embroidery. It is gathered and held by a triple row of wax orange blossoms and buds. She wears satin t-strap shoes with large crystal buckles on the vamp.

Breaking the Glass

The Jewish custom of the groom, and more recently the bride and groom, breaking a glass underfoot at the end of the marriage ceremony is said to be symbolic of the destruction of the first Temple in Jerusalem and reminds the couple and their guests of the fragility of life and relationships. It is also said that although elementally the glass is unchanged (the glass is still glass) the structure of the glass has been completely, and irreversibly changed and so are the lives of the bride and groom forever changed by marriage.

This bride wears a straight, shapeless silk dress with a scoop neck, short sleeves, and large crystal beads down the midline to the hem. Her silver brocade shoes have a large self-material buckle on the vamp and must have been very expensive in 1922 – certainly, this is a bride of some substance.

Her cathedral-length tulle veil forms a corona at the back of her head and is held by an impressive diadem of lace trimmed in pearls. She wears a long string of pearls and opera-length gloves. Her waterfall bouquet of pale roses and fern contains over two-dozen, large, white roses. Note the groom's bowler hat, which he holds at his side.

The Bridal Bag

During the wedding reception, many Italian and Italian-American brides practice the custom of "a buste" in which the bride carries "la borsa", a satin, drawstring bag often with lace edging. "A buste" in Italian means "in envelopes" and "la borsa" or "the bag" is meant to hold gifts of money. Wedding guests slip their gift (envelopes or wedding cards with money enclosed) into the bag as the bride and groom make their rounds. This is a charming tradition that may be incorporated into any wedding and certainly a more personal method of receiving gifts than the "mailbox" or gift table now seen at many receptions.

On July 1, 1923, Josephine married Anthony at Mt. Carmel Church in Harlem, New York. In addition to the bride and groom, there were 21 attendants; each of the women attendants wore a different dress. The wedding party of relatives and friends consisted of: a maid of honor, eight bridesmaids (each wearing a different style dress), a best man, eight ushers and three flower girls. Such a large wedding party ensured that no friends or branch of the family were overlooked.

This wedding party is a classic example of the versatility of bridal headwear seen during the 1920s. There was no set rule as to which headpiece a bride or a bridesmaid could wear. The women all wear either a narrow bandeau or a wider "headache band" with the exception of the bridesmaid standing second from right; she wears a diadem.

A diadem is a tiara-like headpiece that comes to a high point in the front. Some, like this one have a high, soft curve, others are triangular shaped and dramatically pointed. The diadem was the most popular headpiece for brides and bridesmaids during the 1920s.

Spooning

The term "spooning" arises from the ancient Welsh practice whereby a man carved a fancy wooden spoon for the woman he admires. If she wore the spoon on a ribbon around her neck it meant she returned his affection. During the 18th and 19th centuries a popular practice, especially in the United States, was for a man to send a silver, or coin silver spoon engraved with both his and his beloved's initials to the woman he loved as a love token.

The Krenzel

A "krenzel" is the Yiddish word for the "crown" of leaves and flowers that is placed on the head of the mother of the bride if the bride is the last daughter to be married. Once the mother of the bride is thus crowned she becomes the center of a dance called the Mezinke Tanz and is encircled by family and friends who dance around her.

This bride's sheer, silk georgette gown is almost completely obscured by her very elaborate veil and monumental beribboned waterfall bouquet that entirely conceals her torso. The headpiece, a lace cloche cap with a corona of shirred tulle across the crown, sits low on the bride's waved and bobbed hair and gives rise to a magnificent, cathedral-length tulle and lace veil. She wears three rows of pearls.

"The real act of marriage takes place in the heart, not in the ballroom or church or synagogue. It's a choice you make - not just on your wedding day, but over and over again - and that choice is reflected in the way you treat your husband or wife." Barbara de Angelis

Old Shoes

A tradition that is credited to the ancient Assyrians, Hebrews, and Egyptians who used the transfer of footwear in business contracts is one that has been practiced until fairly recent times. This is the custom of the transference of authority over the bride from the bride's father to the groom. Initially it was somewhat contractual but the observance eventually waned and ended as nothing more than a symbol of an archaic custom. The shoe was a symbol of possession and authority, and when a girl married; her father gave her old shoes to the groom to signify that his authority over her was now transferred to his son-in-law. The groom would tap the bride on the head with the shoe to emphasize his new responsibility and the transference of authority from the bride's father to him.

During the 1920s, waistlines dropped, hemlines rose, and hats were worn low on the brow. This young bride, married in 1924, wears a calf-length, bugle-beaded georgette dress with a sheer chiffon overskirt. The headpiece sits low on the brow and is liberally decorated in wax orange blossoms and buds. Her tulle veil is chapel-length, her stockings pale, and her satin shoes have single button crossover straps.

"Love does not dominate; it cultivates." Johann Wolfgang von Goethe (1749 – 1832)

Teresa chose a classic flapper style dress when she married Paul in 1923. The silk georgette dress has a straight cut, tubular, hip-length bodice and calf-length tiered skirt with shirring on the skirt and at the round neckline. In place of the traditional bridal veil and headpiece she wore a frill-edged, brimless helmet cloche decorated by a large ribbon. Her shoes are silk as are her stockings. A waterfall beribboned bouquet of fern and white roses are her only concession to tradition.

More on the Wedding Cake

An old practice in England was to bake a ring in the wedding cake as a symbol of the happiness of the wedding day. A year of constant happiness was predicted for the guest who received the piece of cake that contained the ring. Wedding cakes are an important part of the wedding feast or reception. The cutting and sharing of the wedding cake by the bride and groom symbolizes the "breaking of bread" with their guests.

Many superstitions surround the wedding cake. It was considered unlucky for a bride to bake her own wedding cake. It was believed that a bridesmaid who carried a piece of wedding cake in her pocket until the bride and groom return from their honeymoon would soon be married. A bride who tastes the wedding cake before it is cut will lose the fidelity of her husband. A woman who places a piece of wedding cake under her pillow for seven nights will, on the seventh night, dream of the man she will marry.

This remarkably impressive cathedral-length train of many, many yards of lace and tulle consists of two wide panels of tulle separated by a wide, central panel of fine, Limerick-like lace. The veil, bouquet, and train almost completely obscure the bride's faille dress. A smooth fitted cap of lace is gathered at the back of her head and falls in long, pointed lace folds. Gathered lace and tulle protrude from beneath the lace cap to bust-length in front and thigh-length behind. The large, satin-beribboned bouquet of hundreds of lily-of-the-valley was hardly something a bride could carry about for too long.

When this woman was married in 1924 a wealthy bride's wedding ensemble could cost more than a moderately priced automobile of the day.

During the late 1840s Rachel Ann Voorhis presented this hair bracelet engraved with her initials to Captain Jacob J. Westervelt whom she married on April 27, 1854; the bracelet contained his photograph. He was killed aboard his ship the U. S. S. Underwriter during the civil war on February 02, 1864. His last letter to his wife, written hours before his death, ended: "I leave today nothing more but my love to you and the children. Yours Ever, Jacob."

Made in the Shade: chuppahs and umbrellas

Jewish weddings, by tradition, are held beneath a chuppah - a tent supported by four poles. This chuppah symbolizes the new couple's dwelling together and the bringing of a wife into her new husband's home. Many Chinese couples are married beneath an umbrella, which serves to honor and protect the newly married couple now embarking on a new journey together through life.

This satisfied looking bride wears a short-sleeve, below-the-knee satin dress (very popular in 1925) with a scoop neck, fine lace overskirt, pale stockings, satin shoes, and a long strand of pearls. The lace cloche cap with its high, wire boned, lace corona trimmed in wax orange buds completely demands the viewer's attention. The cap sits low on her brow and tightly covers her waved and bobbed hair. The lace of the corona and cap continues as trim for the cathedral-length tulle veil.

Happy expressions, such as the one on this beautiful bride with the clef chin, have, by this time, almost become the norm.

"Sympathy constitutes friendship; but in love there is a sort of antipathy, or opposing passion. Each strives to be the other, and both together make up one whole." Samuel Taylor Coleridge

Ring Bearer's Pillow

The pillow on which the ring is borne has its origins in coronation ceremonies. Coronation crowns are traditionally carried upon pillows, and so, bearing something upon a pillow has come to symbolize a very ceremonial way in which to present precious articles.

Large is the word to describe every aspect of this wedding party from the number of attendants to the hats, the bouquets, and the largest ribbons and bows seen thus far.

The bride wears a shin-length gown of deeply tiered lace with a V-shaped neckline and a waist and bodice that is wholly obscured by her enormous, beribboned, waterfall bouquet of fern (*fascination*), lily of the valley (*return of happiness*), and pale roses (*love, happiness, worthiness*). Her heavily embroidered, cathedral-length tulle veil has a circular, scalloped hem and is one with the embroidered tulle cap decorated on each side with large clusters of fabric orange blossoms.

The bridesmaids wear sleeveless, V-neck, shin-length gowns with scalloped hemlines, satin boulevard-heel shoes, silk stockings, and large, wide-brimmed, silk capeline hats. They carry large bouquets of dark red roses (*love, desire, respect, courage*) and fern (*fascination, sincerity, shelter*) and wear outstanding orchard corsages (*beauty*). All the women wear pearls.

The young attendants are classic examples of the 1920s notion of a flower girl and ring bearer, who carries an elaborate, lace trimmed, beribboned pillow.

This captivating bride's expression leaves no doubt as to her feelings on her wedding day. Her smile is not only an expression of her joy; it might also symbolize the small tastes of freedom women were now beginning to experience. A mere twenty, even ten, years earlier a woman would not have displayed such unconcealed emotion in a photograph, let alone to a professional photographer.

The new, shorter dress style is also a sign of the changing times. She wears a lustrous satin dress with a deep scallop hem. The skirt has panniers that end in long, narrow, free hanging panels, and an elegant cathedral-length, Watteau, panel train, which falls from the shoulder. The bodice is satin at the sides and satin with overall beading from the neck to the waist at front and back.

Her butterfly-shaped headdress fastens a chapel-length tulle veil, which she wraps around herself like wings. The tulle is so sheer that the details of her dress, even the beading on the bodice, can be seen through it without difficulty. She wears opera-length gloves and pointed, satin shoes.

Perhaps the most appealing feature of this photograph from 1926 is the unusual and alluring pose this bride assumed at a time when a woman's individuality was little more important than a precocious child's feelings. The photograph conveys the personality of a woman, who, when dissected aesthetically, may not fit the definition of beauty, but who is made beautiful and compelling by the fascinating and confident image she projects.

"Love is something eternal; the aspect may change, but not the essence."
Vincent van Gogh (1853 – 1890)

The Nose Knows

The nose knows, or the way to the heart is through the nostrils. How often do we see a couple and wonder what their attraction for each other could possibly have been? The answer may be explained by pheromones. The effects that smell and odor have on attraction have been know since ancient times when people bathed in essence laced waters and aromatic oils. In Medieval times people would tuck a peeled apple or handkerchief in their armpit and, once it had been adequately saturated in their essence, offer it as a love token to the object of their affection. This gives an entirely new meaning to the expression, "An apple a day…"

Was this practice based solely on custom or biology? The answer, it appears, is biology. In 1986 Dr. Winifred Walker of the Monell Chemical Senses Center in Philadelphia described the benefits of male pheromones on women after she successfully isolated the pheromones. Briefly put, Dr. Walker, after collecting male underarm sweat, mixing it with alcohol, and dabbing it on the upper lip of women with irregular menstrual cycles, found that the male scent increased the woman's sexual desire, improved fertility, and helped normalize irregular cycles.

This bridal party is right up to the minute in terms of the fashion of their day. The bride wears a below-the-knee silk dress with straight lines and a scallop hem. The dress is veiled in sheer, figured chiffon, has narrow floral bands from shoulder to waist, and large stylized flowers on the skirt. Her chapel-length tulle veil with boudoir-style cap is fastened by a band of wax orange buds and blossoms.

Her bridesmaids wear large, silk-crepe, capeline hats and dresses of different styles: bugle-beaded, below-the-knee silk georgette, and a below-the-knee satin dress with sheer georgette veiling decorated by pearl and ostrich feather medallions at the hem and right shoulder.

This bride combines traditional lace with modern style in this eye-catching sleeveless, pearl studded wedding dress of floral patterned silk crepe de Chine. The bodice has a very low scoop neckline outlined in pearls and a fancy lace yoke modesty panel. The knee-length skirt is veiled in an elegant lace overskirt to below-the-knee length. She wears sheer, silk stockings, round-toed, silver satin shoes, and a string of pearls. The combination of no sleeves, a low neckline, a high hemline, and sheer stockings was referred to as "the nude look."

Her cathedral-length tulle veil is edged in lace and trails from a rolled-brim tulle cloche cap decorated by a very ornate diadem-shaped crown of wax orange buds. She carries a beribboned bouquet of fern (*fascination, sincerity, shelter*) and organza peonies (*happy marriage, healing*) with trailing ribbons of knotted fern.

It was not at all unusual, indeed quite common, for the modern bride of the 1920s to forego wearing her mother or grandmother's gown in favor of the stylish short styles of the day. Many, however, maintained wedding tradition to a degree by incorporating heirloom lace from their mother or grandmother's wedding gown or veil into their "new" style wedding gowns.

Jumping the Broom

Jumping the broom is an African American tradition with origins in Africa.
A broom, which represents a clean sweep of the past and all former concerns, is placed before a newly married couple who step, or jump over the broom to begin a new life as partners. The jumping can take place immediately after the ceremony while stepping off the altar, or as the bride and groom enter the reception hall, or even when they enter their home for the first time as husband and wife. Although any broom will do, a nice touch would be to buy a rush broom in an arts and crafts store and decorate it with real or artificial flowers that match those in the bride's bouquet. After the ceremony this wedding broom can be used to decorate the bride's home and later passed along to her children for their weddings. Traditions have to begin somewhere, why not with your own wedding? This is a charming ritual that anyone can use in their marriage ceremony or celebration.

"She had a womanly instinct that clothes possess an influence more powerful over many than the worth of character or the magic of manners." Lousia May Alcott (1832 – 1888)

The Toast

Although the practice of marking or commemorating an event with the sharing of a drink has long been practiced throughout the world the toast signified by the clinking of glasses is a tradition that was established in the western world. Perhaps the clinking of the glasses is a vestige of a time when poisoning was not so uncommon. One supposition is that prior to drinking, the wine in each glass would be mixed, resulting in a clinking sound. The term "toast" as a gesture of good will may have originated during the sixteenth century when wine was commonly used to drink to someone's health and vigor. Wine during that time usually contained heavy sediment, which made drinking the gritty mixture a bit unpleasant unless it was somehow filtered. Someone had the brilliant idea of putting a piece of toasted bread over the sediment that had settled at the bottom of the glass; this toast provided an adequate filter. The term "toast" may also have its roots in the practice of flavoring wine with toasted spice bread during the seventeenth century.

The *International Handbook on Alcohol and Culture* reports that toasting *"is probably a secular vestige of ancient sacrificial libations in which a sacred liquid was offered to the gods: blood or wine in exchange for a wish, a prayer summarized in the words 'long life!' or 'to your health!'"*

This lace covered, brimless cloche cap with a wire-boned, lace corona commands the viewer's complete attention. The cap, which lacks the traditional veil, is remarkable in its style and shape.

The gown has a silk crepe, short-sleeved bodice with a scoop neckline and a bouffant dress flounced in V-shaped tiers of lustrous slip satin. She wears elbow-length gloves, round-toed, silver satin shoes, and a pearl necklace with an elaborate pearl drop. Tacked to her right shoulder is a silk rose and she carries a beribboned bouquet of fern and mixed color roses dripping with near transparent streamers.

145

Broken Dishes and Spit

Upon returning home after their weddings many nineteenth century English brides would throw a plate with a piece of wedding cake on it out the window. If the plate broke the bride was assured a happy future with her new husband, if the plate did not break it was taken as a very unlucky sign for the couple's future happiness together.

Spitting on the bride to insure good luck has been a practice in Greece and in the Massai tribes of Kenya for generations. During a Greek wedding ceremony it is not unusual to see people spitting on the bride as she passes down the aisle. The Massai bride is spat upon by her father before she leaves with her new husband; he spits on her head and breasts.

Fashions during the late 1920s heralded the long, slinky look that dominated the 1930s. During the late 1920s hemlines once again dropped low. This wedding party from 1927 is outfitted in elegant, formal attire. The bride's ankle-length, bias-cut, satin gown has a low scoop neckline and slightly puffed sleeves. The fitted lace cap has a unique wire-framed, stellar-shaped lace corona decorated with a tulle chou that drapes to her waist. This distinctive lace cap sits back on her head and fashions a charming frame for her face. She carries a massive beribboned bouquet of pale roses and fern and wears a pearl necklace.

The bridesmaids wear floor-length, sleeveless gowns of lace and satin with low scoop necklines. Choux of tulle and tulle veiling are fastened by fancy rhinestone headbands. Shoes of white decorated leather are worn by the women; one pair with a simple black design the other with a buckle and decoration at the vamp. The flower girls are simply attired in above-the-knee length sleeveless dresses with tiered skirts and they carry beribboned baskets of fern and pale roses.

Who Will I Marry?

   Bridal lore held that an unmarried woman who placed a piece of wedding cake beneath her pillow would dream of her future husband that night. An unmarried man who did the same would significantly increase his chances of finding and marrying a suitable mate. A piece of wedding cake was not the only object used to determine the identity of a future mate. Apple stems, seeds and peels were used as well as the petals of flowers, four leaf clovers, mirrors, and even horseshoes and the breast bones of chickens were used to predict one's future true love.

   The style worn by this bride during the late 1920s is classic for the waning years of that roaring decade; a satin bias-cut gown that is mid-calf at front but dips to ankle-length at the back. The gown has a low V-neckline, short cap sleeves, and a wide diagonal hip yoke. The headdress is a neat, off-the-face cloche decorated by wax orange buds and blossoms at the temple; it fastens a cathedral-length tulle veil. Her sheaf bouquet is of baby's breath, fern, and a flower classic for the period; calla lilies. The brocade, round-toe shoes with Louis heels were considered chic footwear for brides.

1930: Long, Lean and Sensuous

Hemlines were once more below the knee in 1929 but with a difference – the classic hemline of 1929, seen in all types of dresses, including those for brides, was an uneven flare that came below the knee in front and was longer, often ankle-length behind. This new, uneven, flared hemline was achieved by the use of hip yokes and cutting of the material on the bias. These dresses were typically form-fitting from hip to mid-thigh or knee before flaring into smooth, wide folds that conveyed an air of graceful, elegant, fluid motion. Women were as likely to marry in their best sleek slipper satin dress of this style as they were to marry wearing the traditional white gown. This was especially so after the Stock Market crash of 1929 and throughout the ensuing Great Depression. Expensive wedding gowns, meant to be worn only once, were a frivolous and costly expenditure during that time. Between 1928 and 1929 the forehead came out of its cloche and bandeau hibernation. Bridal caps were neat, smooth, fitted, usually of lace, and sat back on the head to expose the hairline. They were decorated at the temple with wax orange buds and blossoms or fabric flowers. Tulle veiling was attached at the edges or back of the bridal cap from where it flared into a frothing cascade. Bridal couples continued to assume charming, even intimate poses – a refreshing change from the poses seen prior to the liberating 1920s.

A *hip yoke* is the part of the dress that is fitted at the hips and supports the attached, gathered, flared skirt – a look that de-emphasized the bust.

Bias cut refers to material cut on a bias (along a slant or diagonal line of the weave), which causes it to cling and give a very sensuous look.

Slipper satin is the shiniest satin and is highly reflective, which gives it a fluid appearance with movement

The cake toppers on the previous page show a bride and groom with three attendants. They are made of cloth and are clothed in tulle and crepe paper. This set was purchased in 1929 in New York City by a young bride on the way to her wedding at City Hall. The bride and groom were trying to hail a cab when it began to rain. They stepped inside Dennison's at 411 Fifth Avenue where the bride spotted this set in the window. She paid twenty-cents apiece for them and later that day used them around her cake. Afterward she carefully wrapped them in tissue paper and placed them in a shoe box where they remained for about seventy years.

This image clearly depicts the neat classic look of the bridal headpiece that dominated the late 1920s and early 1930s. The headpiece is an off-the-face, close-fitting cap, usually of lace, decorated at the temple or angle of the jaw with wax buds or fabric orange blossoms. A tulle veil was typically attached to the edge of the cap at the sides and back, but more often only at the back. The charming and intimate pose in this photograph is a refreshing change from the poses seen prior to the mid-1920s. Photography has always, often unintentionally, recorded societal changes including the emergence of women in terms of expression and equality.

"To love someone deeply gives you strength. Being loved by someone deeply gives you courage." Lau Tzu

The First Dance

The first dance between the new bride and groom has its roots in the Anglo Saxon practice of bride by capture. After capturing his bride-to-be the Saxon man would proudly parade his hunting skills and his catch to his friends and kinsman. The clan would gather in a circle and the prospective groom would lead his lady around within the circle so that each of his kinsmen might get a good look at their new relation.

Many brides in the late 1920s considered the traditional white wedding gown and veil not only passé, but also symbolic of a past when brides were chattel and marriages arranged. They wanted newer, up-to-date, emancipated fashions for their walk down the aisle. They wanted a dress of quality, great beauty, and, more importantly in the days of the depression, practicality – a dress that could be worn again.

An extremely popular and classically beautiful style was the satin, bias-cut skirt with an uneven hem and dip in the back. This bride wears just that type of dress, which accentuates the waist and hip with a hip yoke. The dress has short, puff sleeves, a scoop neckline, and is decorated by large fabric flowers at the left hip. She wears satin shoes and a large horsehair hat with a wide, turned-back, transparent brim pinned to the beribboned crown.

"Don't marry the person you think you can live with; marry only the individual you think you can't live without." Dr. James C. Dobson

Flowers

Victorians believed in the language of flowers and most flowers had their own "secret" meaning. Some flowers were sent to arrange rendezvous, others were sent to refuse these amorous offers (the striped carnation is a flower of refusal). It is no surprise then that when choosing her bouquet many brides thought long and carefully about the flowers she chose and the message she wished to convey.

Yes, brides did have facial muscles and during the 1920s they began exhibiting the versatility of those muscles for the camera's lens. The broad smile on the bride in this 1929 photograph leaves no doubt that she is happy to be married. She wears a classic cloche cap with a small, turned-up brim. The silk crepe, double-tiered dress, which has knuckle-length sleeves and a low scoop neckline is fitted at the hip and dips low in the back. Her shoes are high-heeled, dark leather, and she wears a long string of pearls clasped at the throat. This bride seems to have completely shunned the traditional bridal trappings except for the inclusion of her chrysanthemum bouquet (*white for truth, dark for loveliness*), which is itself rather unconventional in shape and foliage. (See the same bride in the following photograph).

One can't help but be happy while looking at the joy on this beautiful young bride's face (also seen in the previous photograph). Her youthful exuberance is timeless, which makes it difficult to imagine that today she would be well over one-hundred years old. It is also difficult not to imagine what became of her or how she spent the rest of her life after leaving on her honeymoon in this decorated automobile. The image leaves you with the hope that she remained as happy as she appears here on her wedding day - a wish for every bride.

Jointed bisque wedding cake topper with crepe paper clothing circa mid-1920s. During the early nineteenth century cake toppers reflected the changes seen in bridal wear and popular fashion. Very often the bride and groom were actually the same figure dressed in different clothing.

By the end of the 1920s short skirts had outlived their brow-raising popularity and dresses were again longer with an emphasis on elegance. This bride wears a long white chiffon taffeta gown with a train. The gown has a round neck, long sleeves and an interesting yoke of circular, pin-tucked pleats. Her small lace cap (somewhat like a Juliet cap) just covers the crown of her head at the back of which can be seen the veil, which is cathedral-length and embroidered at the end in a swirl pattern. She wears gauntlet gloves (considered very chic in 1929) and carries a large bouquet of fern and white lilies, which are symbolic of chastity and virtue.

Her bridesmaid wears a floor-length silk chiffon gown with a double-tiered round cape collar and a row of tiered frills from the waist to the hem at the back. Her large horsehair hat has a turned-back brim, which is tacked to the ribbon bound crown. She wears high-heeled, silk, t-strap shoes and carries a bouquet of fern (*fascination, shelter*) and carnations (*fascination, white for pure love and innocence, red for admiration and yearning*). Both women wear smiles.

After the stock market crash of October 1929, many brides once again married wearing their best in order to avoid the expense of a traditional white gown and its accessories. Reasons of finance, style, or practicality were not the only motivation a bride had for choosing to marry in her best dress instead of the traditional white wedding gown. Women who married for the second time, for whatever reason, wore their best as well. It would have been considered a gross violation of mores for a divorced or widowed woman to wear the traditional white.

This 1930 bride wears a wool crepe dress with wide, loose, three-quarter length sleeves and a cowl neck. A same-material belt with a large, art deco rhinestone buckle belts the dress, and her dark velvet hat is decorated with a large rhinestone clip. She wears a substantial corsage of fern, foil ribbons, and gardenias (*joy*).

Note the beautiful, round-faced watch, engagement ring, and wedding band displayed for the photographer.

During the 1930s Marguerite, a young woman from England chose this elegant gown for the January wedding to her American sweetheart. The gown is composed of graduated, horizontal bands of lustrous satin each wider than the one above. The satin bands alternate with bands of fine net through which can be seen a darker fabric underskirt. The bouffant, floor-length gown has a narrow waist, fitted bodice, short puff sleeves, and a very low sweetheart neckline that is filled in with a dark chemisette.

Her dark velvet aureole cap has a rolled and shirred bumper brim to which is attached a fine flyaway tulle veil and blusher. She wears elbow-length gloves and round-toed satin shoes. The classic, hand-tied, circular bouquet contains an outer rim of finely pleated, stiffened, sheer organza, then a circle of greens and lily of the valley, and finally, a dome of tightly packed roses surrounding a rosebud center. The bouquet is dripping in bows and long satin streamers knotted with lily of the valley.

"Let the husband render unto the wife due benevolence: and likewise also the wife unto the husband." The Bible: 1 Corinthians 7:3

The Language of Flowers

Angel Vine - intoxication
Asparagus fern - sincerity
Baby's breath - everlasting love
Cactus - warmth, enduring love, something the Southwestern bride may want to consider
Calla lily - beauty, elegance, ardor
Carnations - innocence, distinction
Chrysanthemum - white for truth, dark for loveliness
Daisy - innocence
Delphinium - heavenly light
Fern - wisdom, fascination
Forget-me-not - loving remembrance
Gardenia - joy
Honeysuckle - boundless affection
Hyacinth - loveliness, youth, constancy, benevolence
Ivy - friendship in adversity, fidelity
Jasmine - affection, intensity in love
Laurel leaves - victory, achievement
Lavender - from the Latin word "to wash" it was used to scent bridal beds, bodies, and clothing. It is also said to have the power to wash away worries about the wedding night.
Lilly of the Valley - virtue, return of happiness, tears of the Virgin Mary
Lily - purity, sweetness, innocence
Marigolds - sacred affection, protection of young women
Myrtle leaves - love, fertility, youth, peace, wedded bliss
Oak leaves - wealth – a nice touch for the autumn bride's bouquet
Orange blossoms - beauty, fertility
Pansy - from the French word for thought "pensée", denotes love of a sweetheart
Peonies – pale denotes shyness, in general peonies symbolize humility
Periwinkle - sweet memories
Roses - red denotes deep love and passion, white for pure love, pink for romance and tender feelings, orange for vigor and vitality, something which may help make your decision when choosing a flower for your groom's boutonniere
Stephanotis - married bliss
Sweet pea - bliss
Tulips - perfect love
Vines - flowering vines for fidelity
White Carnations - pride, beauty, deep love
Zinnias - fond memory, lasting affection

The Language of Herbs

Dill - promotes desire
Mint - heightens amorous feelings
Parsley - increases fertility
Rosemary – is an herb that has held a place in the wedding bouquet for centuries. The ancient Greeks believed rosemary had the power to enhance memory and by Medieval times it was the symbol of remembrance and was used at all wedding festivals in bouquets, drinks, bridal crowns, and kissing knots. In the early sixteenth century Sir Thomas Moore wrote about rosemary as "…an herbe sacred to remembrance, and therefore to friendship." It has since been used in bridal bouquets.
Sage - wisdom
Sesame - increased fertility
Sweet Basil - good luck

During the 1930s, especially as a result of the economic depression, brides abandoned traditional style wedding gowns in favor of beautiful, fashionable dresses that could be worn for other events. As a result it is often difficult to determine if a photograph from that era is a bride or a bridesmaid.

Veil Lengths

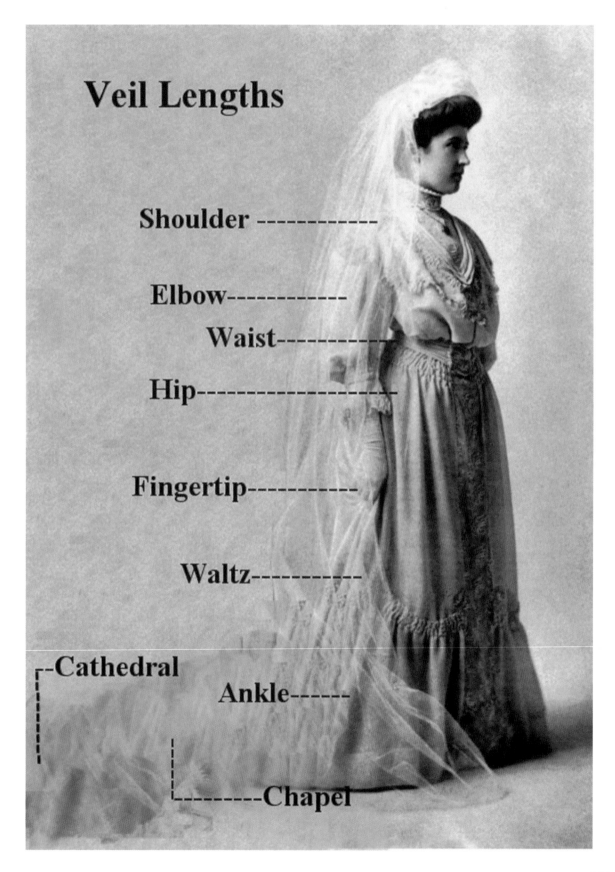

Shoulder -----------

Elbow-----------

Waist----------

Hip-----------------

Fingertip-----------

Waltz-----------

Cathedral

Ankle------

Chapel

Train Lengths

Cathedral

Chapel Court

Sweep

During the wedding ceremony two individuals say "I do" and some may joke that it's probably the last thing they'll agree on for the next thirty years. Differences of opinion, however, often serve to strengthen a relationship with new and balanced perspectives.

When two people wed they promise to love, honor, and cherish. What they don't promise is to surrender their own ideas, individuality, and identities. Conceptually two become one and although that unity is probably the key to a successful marriage it is not the only ingredient. The ways in which you celebrate that "oneness" are no more important than the ways in which you respect each other's differences, ideas, and opinions. A wedding joins hands and hearts, not brains - and that is the alchemy.

A successful marriage is a strange duality, two become one while remaining two, an intangibility whose reality is only as powerful as your faith allows. Cherish unity, respect individuality.

Be kind to each other, not only when things are going well - that's easy, be kind when you are too tired, or too busy, or when you feel like throwing dishes. Listen, protect, and defend each other, and look forward to ending each day in each other's company.

Ostentatious displays of love are unnecessary; it's the thousands of little things that will endure, the daily things you do out of love and kindness - these will endure and give your love a new and stronger direction. Doing the laundry or cooking a meal can sometimes be a more romantic gesture than a dozen roses or a new golf club (though these can't hurt). Learn when to speak and when to bite your tongue and recognize that sometimes pride can be a costly piece of ground.

May your wedding day be the beginning of a story with a very beautiful ending.

Printed in Great Britain
by Amazon